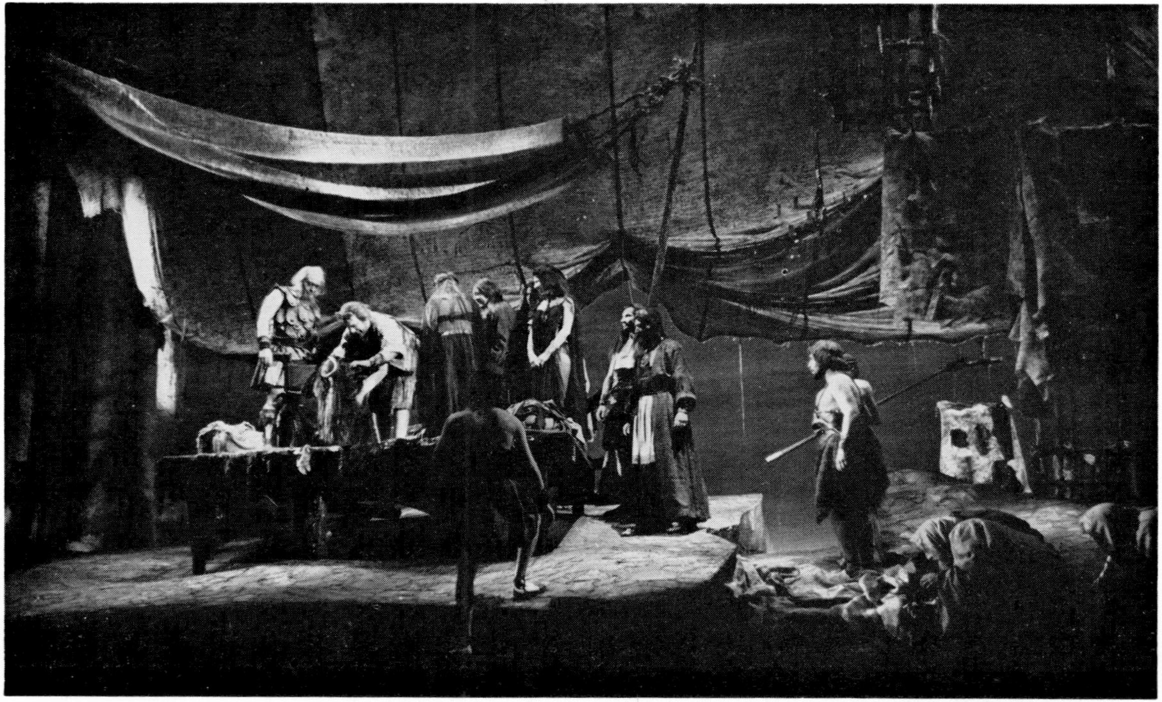

PHOTO BY SHELDON SECUNDA

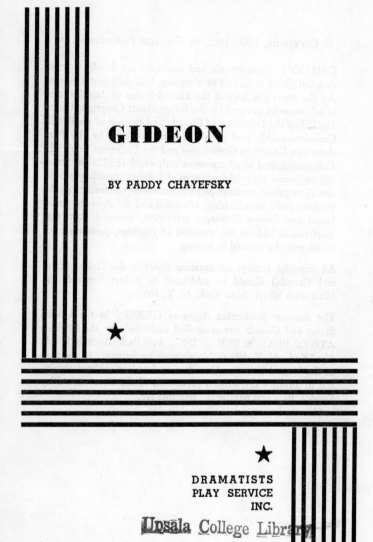

GIDEON

BY PADDY CHAYEFSKY

★

★

**DRAMATISTS
PLAY SERVICE
INC.**

GIDEON was presented by Fred Coe and Arthur Cantor at the Plymouth Theatre in New York City on November 9, 1961. It was directed by Tyrone Guthrie; the settings and lighting were by David Hays; costumes by Domingo A. Rodriguez; produced in association with Carnegie Productions, Inc. The cast, in order of appearance, was as follows:

JOASH	Mitchell Jason
HELEK	Martin Garner
ABIMELECH	Victor Kilian
JETHER	Robert Weiss
GIDEON	Douglas Campbell
ANGEL	Fredric March
SHILLEM	Eric Berry
JAHLEEL	David Hooks
HEZEKIAH	Alan Manson
MALCHIEL	Mark Lenard
PURAH	George Segal
ZEBAH	Alan Bergmann
ZALMUNNA	Paul Marin
SHETHULAH	Edward K. Holmes
OZNI	David Hooks
ORPAH	Lorraine Egypt
WOMEN OF MANASSEH AND SUCCOTH	Florence Anglin, Anna Berger, Bathsheba Garnett, Gubi Mann, Ilene Tema
SOLDIERS	Bernard Chessler, Tom Klunis, Amnon Meskin, Meir Ovadia

TIME: 1100 B.C.

ACT I

SCENE 1: The tent of Joash
SCENE 2: A hill at Harod
SCENE 3: Near the ford at Beth-Barah

ACT II

SCENE 1: Near the city of Succoth
SCENE 2: The tent of Joash

3

PRODUCTION NOTE

The biblical epigrams which appear at the beginning of each scene are an integral part of the play and should be utilized in production. It is suggested that they be placed on signs or boards, which can then be lowered from the flies or brought in from the wings. This should be done during the period between scenes.

4

GIDEON

ACT I, SCENE 1

"Now the angel of the Lord came and sat under the oak at Ophrah, which belonged to Joash, the Abiezrite, as his son Gideon was beating out wheat in the wine-press to hide it from the Midianites."

ACT I

SCENE 1

TIME: June, 1100 B.C.
The scene is the hill country of Manasseh, west of the Jordan River in Biblical Palestine.
Stage R. is a wine-press. Upstage of the wine-press is a terebinth tree. Upstage C. is a crude stone sacrificial altar. Stage L. is a black Bedouin-like tent.
AT RISE: *A man with a black beard and almost entirely enshrouded in long black Mosaic robes is leaning against the terebinth tree. He is an angel.*
Enter the elders from stage R., Joash, Abimelech, and Helek, followed by a frightened boy of twelve, whose name is Jether. The elders are all in their sixties. They wear variously-colored robes. They hurry to the stone altar upstage C., lift their faces and begin to wail softly. They beat their breasts, pour ashes from the altar's hearth over their heads.

JOASH. (*Crying out.*) O, Mighty Ba-al! Progenitor of Oxen! Rider of the Clouds and the Bringer of Rain! Hear the entreaty of your servant Joash . . .
ABIMELECH. . . . and of Abimelech his kinsman . . .

5

JOASH. Hear the entreaty of Joash of the house of Abiezer of the tribe of Manasseh.

HELEK. O Puissant Ba-al!

JOASH. O Mighty Ba-al! Hear the voice of your servant Joash!

ABIMELECH. Do not ignore Abimelech his kinsman.

HELEK. Nor Helek son of Zoar.

JOASH. All-potent Father! O Mighty Ba-al! The Midianites are upon us again! (*The four men burst into fresh wailing. They beat their breasts. They pour ashes on their heads. They rend their garments.*) We have seen their tents in Gilead on the other side of the Jordan River. Every year, for eight years, they have thundered up from the desert of Havilah, one hundred thousand swarming nomads, their camels and their flocks. Like locusts, they devour everything before them, the harvests of Reuben, the barley of Gad. And now they are here again, this vast savage multitude. From our hills, we have seen the glint of their ear-rings and the golden cresents that hang from their camels. As far as the eye can see, their black tents darken the land of Gilead. Soon they will cross the Jordan and devour us here.

HELEK. Woe is Manasseh! Woe unto us here in Manasseh!

JOASH. They will take our daughters to be their servants.

ABIMELECH.
O Divine Ba-al! Save us! Redeem us!
Smite them with plagues, smite them with lightning.
Strike with your cudgels.

JOASH.
Give us a hero,
a redeemer, a savior.
Raise up a prince who will lead us in battle!
Raise up a hero!
You donkey! What have you brought here?

(*This last, needless to say, was hardly addressed to Ba-al, but rather to a strapping, good-natured, bearded fellow in his late 30's named Gideon, who has just entered D. R., carrying the carcass of a newly-slaughtered young goat. He pauses at this greeting.*)

GIDEON. Father, I am bringing the sacrifice, as you asked me.

JOASH. A bullock! A bullock! I said to slaughter a bullock, Gideon, not a kid!

GIDEON. Oh, I heard you to say a kid.

ABIMELECH. Oh, let's get on with this sacrifice.

6

JOASH. My son Gideon has brought in a kid instead of a bullock.

ABIMELECH. Well, offer the kid then. We all want to get back to our tents and hide whatever we can before the Midianites come.

JOASH. (*Taking the kid from Gideon and putting it on the altar, muttering. Gideon crosses* D. *and sits on wine press.*) Five sons I had; four were killed by the Midianites, and this is the one who was spared. (*Pulling his knife from its scabbard.*) Now, does anyone remember the ritual we followed last year?

HELEK. It didn't help much last year so I shouldn't worry too much about repeating it exactly.

ABIMELECH. You dip your hand in the blood of the sacrifice and sprinkle it on the horns of the altar and . . .

JOASH. Yes, yes, I remember all that. It's the portion I'm asking about. How much of the animal do we actually offer? Does the right shoulder and upper right joint sound familiar to anyone?

HELEK. No, no, the proper portion for a sacrifice to My Lord Ba-al is the two cheeks, the stomach, the shoulders and all the fat thereof.

JOASH. Oh, I know that's not right.

ABIMELECH. (*Reaching impatiently for the knife in Joash's hand.*) Oh, let me do it.

JOASH. No, I'm chief of the clan.

ABIMELECH. Well, finish up with it then.

JOASH. (*Dipping his hand into the blood of the sacrificial kid and sprinkling some on the ground.*) It's a mangy little animal. Why don't we just offer up the whole kid and be done with it?

ABIMELECH. Good.

JOASH. (*Now rubbing the blood on the tips of the horns of the altar.*) Gideon, while I'm doing this—there are some sheaves of wheat that I brought into the tent. Beat them out and put the threshed wheat in a sack and hide the sack in that cave we used last year.

GIDEON. Yes, father. (*Gideon goes to tent to get wheat, which he ties up.*)

JOASH. (*Now applying some blood to his forehead, the thumb of his right hand, and to the toe of his right foot—He nudges Abimelech.*) You see the point? We shall have to thresh the wheat harvest by hand and in secret. If the Midianites see us threshing the wheat on the hilltop, they will know we have had a good harvest and it shall go all the worse with us.

7

ABIMELECH. Oh, that is true. And I have just sent our cousin Lamech up to the threshing floor on the hill. Gideon, you had better send someone up to the threshing floor straightaway to tell Lamech to come down before the Midianites see him.

GIDEON. Yes, Uncle. (*He turns to the boy Jether.*) Jether, my son, go to the threshing floor and tell Lamech to come down straightaway. (*Jether, far more interested in the ritual at the altar, pays his father no attention.*)

HELEK. (*To Joash.*) You forgot to sprinkle the blood seven times around the altar.

JOASH. No, no, I've already done that.

GIDEON. (*Annoyed at his son's indifference, he appeals to his father.*) Father, he never does what I ask him.

JOASH. (*Peremptorily to the boy.*) Go to Lamech and bring him down from the threshing floor. (*The boy leaps to his charge, exiting* U. *and around the tent.*)

ABIMELECH. What shall we do with the herds this year?

HELEK. Well, let us finish with the prayers, and then we can decide what to do with the women and the cattle.

ABIMELECH. I hear wailing. The women have heard the news. (*Indeed, far offstage* L., *we can hear the keening of Women. Joash turns back to the altar.*)

JOASH. O, My Lord Ba-al, you are god over all other gods. And let the people say . . .

THE OTHER ELDERS. Amen. (*Gideon goes into the tent, and hoists several large sheaves of wheat effortlessly onto his shoulders.*)

JOASH.

You have banished Yam to the waters.

You seize the womb of Anath and you are sire to eagles,

And you are father to the grape.

And let the . . . (*He pauses to watch his son Gideon carrying the sheaves of wheat* U. *and around the tent.*)

Where are you going now?

GIDEON. (*Turning.*) Do you speak to me, father?

JOASH. I said where are you going?

GIDEON. I am taking these sheaves of wheat, as you asked me to, up to the threshing floor on the hill and . . .

ABIMELECH. Up to the threshing floor! You witless ass! You have just sent your son to tell Lamech to come down from the threshing floor!

GIDEON. But, uncle, my father has asked me to thresh these sheaves of wheat . . .

JOASH. I said to beat them out! Beat them out in the wine-press!

GIDEON. (*Utterly confused.*) Beat the wheat out in the wine-press?

HELEK. (*Crossing above altar.*) What a donkey!

JOASH. Gideon, if you go up to the threshing floor, the Midianites will see you. They are only across the river. Do you want them to know we are reaping a good harvest? Go to the wine-press, you goat, and beat out the sheaves with a stick.

(*Enter two women in a state of panic. They wear blue and purple robes.*)

THE WOMEN. Oh, my lord Joash, the Midianites are upon us!

JOASH. Yes, yes, we know about that. We are offering prayers to Ba-al now. (*Abimelech suddenly bolts for the wings.*) Where are you going?

ABIMELECH. I have my own fields to reap! (*He exits.*)

JOASH. (*To the women.*) Foolish ladies, you must get back to your gleaning. (*To Helek, who is also bolting away.*) We haven't finished the prayers!

HELEK. (*Exiting.*) Bother the prayers!

THE WOMEN. See how Israel is brought low, how the elders scurry. As lions shall they revour the daughters of Israel.

JOASH. (*Wearily.*) Oh, it is all too much for me. (*He enters the tent and squats gloomily down on his haunches.*)

GIDEON. (*Calling from the wine-press.*) Shall I continue beating out the wheat, father?

JOASH. Yes! (*Mutters.*) Donkey. (*The women go off. One woman, Tirzah, remains, moving in and out of view in the tent as she gathers the stores of the household and puts them in baskets. A moment of silence, interrupted only by the pounding of Gideon's stick as he beats at the kernels of wheat in the wine-press. The black-bearded Angel, who has been watching it all from the shade of the terebinth tree, now steps forward to Gideon and regards the big fellow, whacking away at the wheat.*)

THE ANGEL. The Lord is with you, O mighty man of valor. (*Gideon, who had not noticed the Angel till now, looks up, a little startled.*) I said, the Lord is with you, O mighty man of valor.

9

(This greeting, needless to say, disconcerts Gideon. He darts a quick look back to the tent to see if anyone is around to take the fellow off his hands. He pounds a few more whacks, then smiles sheepishly at the stranger, raises his hand in a gesture of "Be right back," and shuffles quickly into the tent. His father is squatting unhappily on his haunches in the middle of the tent.)

GIDEON. Father, there is a very strange fellow by our terebinth tree.

JOASH. Well, give him what cakes we have on the hearth and show him the road to Schechem.

GIDEON. *(Hurriedly gathering cakes.)* I was beating the wheat, you see, and this fellow suddenly came up, saying . . . *(He hurries out of the tent, across to the stranger now perched on the edge of the wine-press. He offers the cakes and a skin of water.)* We have only these. We are very oppressed here. But you must hurry south before the Midianites come. I will show you the road. One makes for Schechem and then into Ephraim, and then others will show you the roads to Judah. I must get to my work. I have this wheat to beat here. It is slow business. *(Gideon picks up his beating stick and gets back to his work. But the calm stranger unnerves him. The Angel sits perched on the edge of the wine-press amiably munching the flat cakes he has been given.)* Sir, it is hard for me to do my work if you sit there like that.

THE ANGEL. *(Affably.)* I am the Lord your God, Gideon, who brought you out of the iron furnace of Egypt and delivered you from bondage. *(Gideon considers this announcement for a moment.)*

GIDEON. Well, as you say, sir. Now, let me be about my work.

THE ANGEL. I am the Lord your God, Gideon. I have heard your groans under the Midianite yoke. You have cried out to Ba-al, but it is my ears that heard. My wrath was hot against you, for you have bowed down and served the Amorite gods and the Ba-als of the Canaanites. My name is Jealous, Gideon, for I am a Jealous God; and I have delivered you into the hands of the Midianites. But I have remembered the covenant I made with Jacob and the bargain I struck with Moses, and I will redeem you from the Midianite oppression. For My Name is the Loving God, the Gracious God, the Merciful God, and I have hearkened to your groans. *(This is all a little too much for poor Gideon. He makes a few*

10

half-hearted whacks at the wheat in the wine-press, nods his head nervously a few times.)

GIDEON. *(Mutters.)* Excuse me. *(He turns and shuffles back across stage to his father's tent and goes in again.)* It is a very strange stranger, indeed, father. He seems a Hebrew from the cut of his beard, but I—it would be better if you came forth and dealt with him.

JOASH. *(In despair.)* Leave me be, Gideon. *(Gideon nods nervously and takes a few tentative steps out of the tent and would perhaps have made his way back to the wine-press, but he is petrified into a halt by the sudden booming of the stranger's voice. The Angel is now standing in all his black majestic height, and he roars out in volcanic tones.)*

THE ANGEL. I am the Lord your God who brought you out of the house of Egypt! With signs and wonders I delivered you from bondage! Ten plagues I hurled at Pharaoh to awe you with my might. I drove back the sea with a strong east wind, and Israel walked through the waters! The horse and the rider I cast into the sea, but you walked through water! Would that not be a sign enough? Would that not be wonder enough? But you are a stubborn people! From that day to this have you rebelled against the Lord! Did I not rain bread from the heavens? Did I not strike water from the rock at Horeb? How long will you murmur against me? I shattered the walls of Jericho with trumpets. Thirty-one kings with their cities and walls did I give into your hand! But this mighty God was not enough for you! A cult of whores did you require! Mincing priests with crushed testicles! You have made cuttings in your skin and tattoos upon your brows! You have reveled before eyeless gods! You have debauched before stumps of trees! You are a stiff-necked people! You have done evil in mine eyes! *(Gideon, now thoroughly unnerved by what seems a raging lunatic, looks back to the tent to see why his father and wife haven't come running out at this outburst. But the two people in the tent do not seem to have heard.)*

GIDEON. *(Nervously.)* Sir, I do not know why you are so enraged.

THE ANGEL. Gideon, do you not know me? It is hardly four generations since Moses. Do not the young men know my name any more? I am your Lord Yahweh, the Kinsman of Jacob, who was the father of all the houses of Israel.

11

GIDEON. I have heard the old men talk of My Lord Yahweh.

THE ANGEL. Well, I am he.

GIDEON. I shall not say you are not.

THE ANGEL. I tell you I, even I, am He!

GIDEON. Pray, sir, do not shout.

THE ANGEL. (*Crossing* L.) What a stiff-necked fellow you are!

GIDEON. (*Thoroughly distressed, crosses* U. C.) What would you have me say? I am a poor farmer, beating out wheat in his wine-press. Suddenly, a black-bearded stranger appears at my elbow and shouts at me: "I am your God!" Well, I find this all an unusual business. I do not hold everyday traffic with gods. I said: "Very well." What else should I have said? And you have abused me roundly and hold me back from my pressing work.

THE ANGEL. (*Sitting down,* L.) I did not mean to discomfort you.

GIDEON. And now that I am put to it, I will tell you plainly— (*Crosses to the Angel.*) I do not believe in gods. I am not all as witless as my fellows sometimes think me. I have thought about these matters lately, and I do not believe in gods. You say that you are the god, Yahweh. The fact is, sir, in these parts, you are but a minor divinity. When I was a boy, you were more highly thought of, I think. But we Abiezrites are poor men, hill farmers. Our soil is hard, and we must pray for fertility, so we adopted a goddess with breasts and a womb, Ishtar—a sportive lady, I must say; her festivals are lively times. (*Crossing to wine-press.*) A farmer, you see, needs a romping god. And Yahweh, as I recall, was grim. Oh, sir, we have had all manner of gods here—the Bull-El, Yam, Mot, pin-breasted Ashtartes, Anu, Anath, the Mother Goddess of the wonderful womb, and now we have added the rain Ba-al of Beth-shean! And to all these gods I gave my full and primitive awe. (*Crossing back to the Angel and stooping to talk to him.*) I truly, truly served them. For I am a child in many ways and truly though the wind did love me, and that the thunder was angry at something I did, and that I sliced our poor Lord Ba-al in half as I sickled my wheat, for such is the story, you know, that Ba-al dies each year at harvest. How I wailed as I reaped! I truly truly thought the air was cluttered with fierce powers. (*Crosses to altar.*) But lately I have come to wondering.

THE ANGEL. Gideon . . .

GIDEON. (*Indicating the sacrificial kid.*) What god will eat this sacrifice? Only that black bird. You say god to me, but I am a farmer, sir; I know a crow for a crow. A carrion crow is not much of a god really; I can chase him away with a stick.

THE ANGEL. Dear Gideon . . .

GIDEON. I have never asked of any god more than my own, that my trees bear olives, that my ewes bear lambs, the natural increase of things, no special favor. I did ask for seven sons; I have but one.

THE ANGEL. (*Crosses to Gideon.*) You shall have seventy sons, I promise you. And I shall redeem you from the Midianites.

GIDEON. Perhaps so. But lately, as I say, I have come to wondering.

THE ANGEL. Let us be friends, Gideon. For I am, in truth, the Lord your God, and I would have you believe in me. (*There is something so gentle about the black-bearded stranger that Gideon must look at him.*) The Lord is with you, O mighty man of valor. (*Gideon looks quickly away, then squats on his haunches in the manner of the East.*)

GIDEON. If the Lord is with us, sir, then why are we as we are? In my time, it has always been hard for a Hebrew. (*The Angel now squats beside Gideon, as two Oriental farmers might sit for a chat.*)

THE ANGEL. Come, we will talk as kinsmen, for I am the first of your tribe. I like you, Gideon; you are a straightforward man.

GIDEON. Well, you are quick to temper, I see, but there is a sweetness in you.

THE ANGEL. Then, we are friends.

GIDEON. Brothers, since you say so.

THE ANGEL. My brother then, you are a farmer. You know the ways of covenants. When you sell your cow to the caravan and the merchant gives you nothing in exchange, you will rise in anger, I should think.

GIDEON. Aye.

THE ANGEL. It is a breach, is it not?

GIDEON. It is a breach.

THE ANGEL. Well, so it is with me. I have made covenant with the people of Israel, and they have defaulted. I have filled my part of the contract. I promised Jacob I would make of him a great people, and indeed I did. Jacob was but a wandering Aramaean with a household of seventy people when I sent him down into Egypt. And when I led them out of the land of Egypt, the house of Jacob had become six hundred families, rich with flocks and servants. And I gathered the whole full twelve tribes of them at Mount Nebo by the Jordan River. And I put the matter to them plainly there. "Look here," spoke I, "let us renew this covenant of ours, so that things are clear between us. I shall give this land across the Jordan to you, and you shall prosper there. Your part of the bargain is simple enough. You shall not bow down to any other god. I am the Lord your God, and there is no other god. You shall not serve any other god." Could it have been more plainly stated?

GIDEON. No, it was plainly said.

THE ANGEL. Well, after Moses came Joshua, and after Joshua, there rose a new generation in Israel who knew not the Lord, and they played the harlot after the Amorite gods. And such gods, really! A stone lady with a bulbous belly! As you say, with more colorful rites than mine perhaps, but I really did think you Hebrews were a cleverer breed than that. Do you really think if you lay with a priestess, your seed will fecundate barley? (*Rising.*) Come, Gideon, this is merely magic and not fitting for a noble house. It is beyond my understanding—really it is!—what you see in these other gods. The men of Sumer pray to the moon, but your god made the moon and many moons like it. The Philistines bow down to a flea, and the Egyptians—oh, well, the Egyptians will pray to anything. Cats, fish, vermin, frogs, rams, bulls, asps and adders, anything really. (*Crossing* U. L. C.) But your god is no cat. Nor can his likeness be chipped from stone. Not by gold nor red carbuncle can your god be wrought. Your god is beyond dimension. Your god, oh Hebrew, is beyond all other gods. Your god is all. Your god is everything. I am what is. I am the Lord! What was it we were talking of?

GIDEON. You were saying our fathers bowed down to other gods.

THE ANGEL. (*Crossing* D. R. C.) Your fathers indeed! Have *you* not bowed down to Marduk? And now it is Ishtar and the rain Ba-al of Beth-shean. And so I have given you into the hands of the Midianites. (*He has risen now to his full god-like majesty. His voice booms out.*) This one last time shall I redeem you! This one last time, ye Hebrews! (*Gideon looks nervously around, surprised that nobody seems to hear the Angel.*) But if you break faith with me one more time, then cursed shall you be in the city and cursed shall you be in the field! You shall serve your enemies in nakedness!

14

I shall make brutes of you! Your women shall eat their own after-birth! Your men shall eat their sons in hunger. Among all nations, you shall find no rest! For I am the Lord! I am the Lord! I am the Lord! (*He is abruptly affable again, sits* D. C.) I shall raise up from among you a redeemer, and he shall deliver you from the Midianites.

GIDEON. (*Terrified now.*) How shall we know this redeemer?

THE ANGEL. I shall come to him in the guise of a stranger, and I shall say unto him: "The Lord is with you, O, mighty man of valor." (*Gideon nods his head slowly. Then he scowls as he begins to get the drift.*)

GIDEON. I?

THE ANGEL. You shall be the redeemer. Gideon, the son of Joash the son of Abiezer, the son of Gilead, the son of Machir, the son of Manasseh.

GIDEON. You cannot be serious.

THE ANGEL. You shall be the redeemer.

GIDEON. Sir, I am Gideon, the donkey of the clan. (*Crosses to the Angel.*) Ask anyone in Ophrah or on the hills. They shall tell you Gideon is a good enough fellow but an ass. Will you gird a donkey and make him your general? Of course, it is a prank. I am often the butt of such pranks. It is a prank, is it not? Of course. Ho! Gideon the general! What an idea! (*He looks anxiously at the Angel who seems quite serious about the whole matter. Crosses* R.) Sir, I am not a soldier. I wouldn't know which end of the sword is haft.

THE ANGEL. You are a mighty man of valor.

GIDEON. I will not hear any more of this. Really, I . . . the very idea of it has put me at my wit's end. Who will join Gideon's army?

THE ANGEL. The spirit of the Lord shall come upon you, and all Israel shall heed your words.

GIDEON. No, no, sir, I will have no part of this. (*Enter Helek, running from* R. *He is aghast with panic and quite out of breath. The Angel crosses back to the terebinth tree.*)

HELEK. (*Shouting.*) They come! They come! The Midianites come!

ABIMELECH'S VOICE. (*Off* L.) They come! They come! Midian comes!

HELEK. (*Hurrying across to the tent.*) Joash! They come! The shepherds have seen them. They are crossing the river.

15

JOASH. (*At his tent flap.*) Oh, dear me! (*Abimelech comes hurtling in from* L.)

ABIMELECH. They have entered the river! Lamech has seen them from the threshing floor! (*He flings himself down before the altar.*) O! Mighty Ba-al! Let it be quick and done with this year!

JOASH. (*Walking about at a loss.*) Is there time to gather the elders and hold council? (*Far offstage, the women begin a long, ululating wail.*)

THE ANGEL. (*To Gideon.*) Sound the trumpet, man of valor, and gather your army. (*Gideon, who has quite forgotten the stranger in this flurry of panic, turns and regards him blankly.*)

JOASH. (*Shaking with fear and indecision.*) Each man must do what is right in his own eyes. Take what you can and run for the caves.

GIDEON. (*Crosses to Joash.*) Father, I pray you, talk with this stranger, for he frightens me.

JOASH. What stranger?

GIDEON. The man by the terebinth tree.

JOASH. The terebinth tree?

GIDEON. The black-bearded man in the heavy black robes. His hand is outstretched towards us.

JOASH. There is no man by the terebinth tree. Have you lost your wits entirely? (*Gideon turns slowly and stares at the Angel as six women enter, lamenting. Jether, the boy, is with them, terrified and clutching at his mother's robe.*)

THE WOMEN.

> The Kings of Midian ford the Jordan.
> The blood of Gilead drips from their swords.

THE ELDERS. O! We are oppressed!

THE WOMEN.

> The quiet Jordan heaves with waves.
> Thousand on thousand push into the water.
> They come! They come! Midian comes!

THE ELDERS. O! We are wounded and suffer!

THE ANGEL. (*Slowly raising his arm and pointing at Gideon, who is staring with wide-eyed interest at him.*) The spirit of the Lord is upon you, Gideon, and the people shall do as you tell them. (*Gideon turns slowly to the Elders.*)

GIDEON. (*In a state of possession.*)

16

Rise up, ye elders!
Hear the oracle of Gideon, the son, of Joash,
The oracle of the man whose eye is opened!
The Lord of Jacob will redeem you.
The God of Moses is here,
And the Midianites will flee before you seven ways!

(*The Elders look up from their postures of prostration.*)

HELEK. On my head, is this Gideon who prophecies? (*He stands slowly.*)

GIDEON. Sound the trumpet, father! Gather the Abiezrites upon this hill. We shall make war with Midian. (*He seizes his father's sacrificial knife from the altar and, with quick, violent stroke slashes off a section of Helek's robe.*) Send messengers throughout Manasseh. This is what they shall say to the chiefs of Manasseh: "Whosoever does not come out after Gideon, thus shall my sword be brought down upon him." Let them come to me at Harod. There shall we gather an army. The battle shall be met in three days' time. It is the word of the Lord! The trumpet, father! Go fetch the horn and sound it! (*Joash shuffles dumbly into his tent.*) It is the word of the Lord, Helek. (*Helek turns blankly and exits slowly off* R. *To Abimelech.*) Send men servants to Asher, to Naphtali and to Zebulun. Take a yoke of oxen and chop them into pieces, and let your men servants say this to the chiefs: "Whoever does not come out after Gideon, thus shall it be done to his herds." The Lord is with you.

A WOMAN. We have raised up a savior! (*Abimelech nods his head numbly and moves slowly off* L.)

GIDEON. Rise, ye women, and take the aged and children to the stronghold at Schechem. If you come into your monthly weakness in these three days, hide ye from the others, for it is an unclean thing and a bad omen for the battle.

THE WOMEN. (*Rising and intoning.*)
We have raised up a savior.
As a lion does he rise up.
As the wild ox who gores the foe.

(*The women exeunt* L. *The boy, Jether, pauses a moment to regard his father with new interest. Gideon beams at him and the boy exits. Joash comes out of the tent, carrying a large silver trumpet. Gideon stares at him blankly. Now, Joash lets loose a mighty blast. Gideon winces against the loud clarion.*)

JOASH. Shall we sound the horn again, my lord Gideon? (*Gideon turns, startled at this appellation. It pleases him. He looks at the Angel who nods approval. He smiles.*)

GIDEON. Yes, I suppose we had better. (*The fact is, Gideon is very pleased by his new prominence—not quite sure of what has happened but quite pleased nevertheless. Joash sounds the trumpet again, its blast reverberating throughout the theater. Gideon tugs at his beard as he considers the whole remarkable incident favorably. The curtain comes quickly down.*)

END OF SCENE ONE

"Then Jerubaal (that is, Gideon) and all the people who were with him, rose early and encamped beside the spring of Harod; and the camp of Midian was north of them by the hill of Moreh in the valley."

ACT I

Scene 2

The Hill at Harod.

It is late afternoon, three days later.

Upstage is a small spur of a hill. On the spur is Gideon's tent. Downstage of this spur is a second smaller spur. Both these spurs drop away to stage level some feet from the right wing. They are separated by a small defile.

AT RISE: *Gideon is seated downstage against the lower spur. His chin rests gloomily on the palm of his right hand. He is accoutered for war, i.e., he wears a leather corselet which chafes him and a leather baldric studded with iron pieces. In the tent are Shillem the Naphtalite and Jahleel the Zebulunite. Shillem is a grizzled old warrior in his late sixties. He wears a brass cuirass, a wooden helmet with lappets, a leather belt and greaves. He holds a mighty warbow over which he fusses throughout the scene. Jahleel is a man in his fifties, robed and tur-banned. He squats on the carpets. Purah, the man-servant of Gideon, stands guard stage left of the tent. He is armed with a mattock. There is a soldier or two occasionally visible upstage of the tent. Enter two warriors in their late forties. They are Hezekiah and Malchiel. Hezekiah is stripped to the waist and wears a short skirt-like gar-ment that comes to the knees. A pouch of stones, slung over his shoulder, dangles at his hip. He carries a sling. Malchiel wears a knee-length tunic, girdled by a leather belt, and holds a spear. They poke their heads into the tent.*

HEZEKIAH. Peace be with you, is this the tent of Gideon?

SHILLEM. Aye.

HEZEKIAH. We are the captains from Asher. I am Hezekiah of the house of Immah.

MALCHIEL. I am his brother Malchiel of the house of Immah.

SHILLEM. Peace be unto you. I am Shillem, captain of Naphtali, and there sits Jahleel the Zebulunite. (*Purah, at last aware that someone is going into the tent, wheels and brandishes his mattock.*)

PURAH. Who enters the tent of Gideon?

SHILLEM. Rest, rest, sentry, it is only the captains from Asher. (*At Purah's challenge, Gideon stood and peeked over his spur to see the new arrivals. Now he squats again.*) The sentry is an imbecile. I can't step out of this tent to yawn that he doesn't challenge me with his plowshare. Well, how many have you brought with you?

HEZEKIAH. Eight thousand. We are pitched at the southern foot of the hill.

SHILLEM. Eight thousand fishermen from Asher. Well, that brings us now to thirty-two thousand. Well, we are fully met, the hosts of Israel. Thirty-two thousand fishers and husbandmen, armed with mattocks and trammels, a few dirks and darts, harpoons, and some old battleaxes, and flint axes at that. Ha! Not ten archers in the lot. I captained fifty men for Barak when we drove Sisera down the slopes of Tabor into the Kishon River. I mention it, not to bore you with an old warrior's tales, but to say merely that I know the shape of an army, and in truth, captains of Zebulon and Asher, this is an undistinguished garrison we have gathered here. We had expected the men of Asher yesterday. (*Malchiel crosses u. c.*)

HEZEKIAH. Yes, well, it wasn't easy to gather eight thousand men to make war simply because a zealot named Gideon suggested it. I mean, a messenger from Manasseh, brandishing a chopped-up cow, came racing up to the gates of my city, shouting: "Whosoever does not come out after Gideon," and so forth and so forth——well, it's hard to take that sort of thing seriously. I didn't want to come at all, but my brother Malchiel here is a more enthusiastic follower of prophets.

MALCHIEL. (*A fanatic sort.*) We have been told this Gideon is a charismatic man and that he walks in a blinding circle of light.

SHILLEM. Well, not too blinding. I wouldn't put him down as

completely feckless, but he does seem to lack a forceful grip on things.

JAHLEEL. Aye.

SHILLEM. I took our general Gideon up to the crest of this hill this morning. We lay on our bellies and looked down on the Midianite camp in the valley. Their tents stretch ten miles from Shunem to the foothills of Gilboa. If I had to hazard a number, I would count them at a hundred thousand.

JAHLEEL. And there are another twenty thousand Amalekites who ride with them.

SHILLEM. And Gideon prophesied we should smite the Midianites on the third day, and this is the third day.

JAHLEEL. And late in the afternoon of the third day.

SHILLEM. Well, as I say, we looked down upon this awesome multitude, and I said to Gideon: "My general, what plan of battle have you for this?" "I haven't the beginnings of an idea," he said, "have you?" And that was this morning.

HEZEKIAH. You mean we have no plan of battle?

SHILLEM. Absolutely none at all. So I have been conceiving a clever shift or two. Still, we are badly favored in this battle, badly favored. (*He seizes a small branch lying on the table and begins marking the ground at their feet.*) Well, attend. Here we sit on the hill of Harod. Here lay the Midianites in the Valley of Jezreel below. (*The others gather around him. Downstage, the Angel, in excellent spirits, enters. Gideon offers him a quick, sulky look.*)

GIDEON. Where have you been?

THE ANGEL. (*A little surprised at this sulkiness.*) Why are you suddenly so cross? When I left you this morning, you flung yourself at my feet, kissed the hem of my robe and vowed eternal love to me. Now, what occasions this new petulance? Oh, come, Gideon, I have grown so fond of you these past three days. And it is lovely here at Harod at this hour. See all this arbutus; it is a sweet night.

GIDEON. This corselet my uncle gave me chafes.

THE ANGEL. (*Squatting down beside Gideon.*) Oh, take it off. I told you yesterday to take it off. It is much too hot for leather. But you will posture as a general and swagger among the troops. You have your baldric on backwards, I might add.

GIDEON. My manservant Purah said this was the way.

THE ANGEL. And put away that poniard. You will not need it.

21

A handsome one though. Here, let me look at it. Made of an antelope's horn. Is it also your uncle's?

GIDEON. Yes.

THE ANGEL. Very handsome.

GIDEON. The old man Shillem of Naphtali is driving me out of my wits.

THE ANGEL. A vain old man, why do you listen to him?

GIDEON. He keeps clutching my arm and saying: "What have you in the way of a battle plan?" Well, what am I to say? The men of Asher have finally come. Their captains sit in my tent now. "What is the plan of battle?" they shall say. And what am I to answer? The people shout at me as I walk among the tents: "We've left half a harvest in the field. The first grapes will be ripening in a week! We want to be home!" "The Lord of Moses is with you," I answer, "and you shall not fear." Well, I shall have to have something cleverer to say than that, for they grumble a great deal. I said we would engage the Midianites in three days' time, and it is the third day now. And you went off this morning, and here it is dusk. I've been looking for you all through the hills. And you say wherefore do I sulk? (*Crosses* c. *and sits on step.*)

THE ANGEL. You shall have your battle plan. Have no fear.

GIDEON. Why have you kept it secret?

THE ANGEL. (*Crosses to Gideon.*) You never asked me for it. You have been sporting among the people, playing the prince. I watched you shout orders from your tent and gravely scratch maps on the ground. This rodomontade was your diversion; I would not spoil it for you. And I meant you also to know your own incompetence. It shall not be said, when this victory over Midian is won, that it was won by Gideon or any other general. This victory shall be mine. It shall be a miracle. It shall be clear to all Israel that only the hand of God delivered them.

GIDEON. Pray, sir, what is the plan?

THE ANGEL. You shall require three hundred lamps, each filled with an hour's oil.

GIDEON. Three hundred lamps?

THE ANGEL. And three hundred horns.

GIDEON. What manner of horns?

THE ANGEL. Any manner so long as each can blow a loud blast. Go see to these requisitions quickly. It is dusk now, and night falls abruptly in June.

GIDEON. Pray, sir, these three hundred lamps—what is the reason for these three hundred lamps and three hundred horns?

THE ANGEL. (*Crosses to top of defile.*) Yes, another thing. The Midianites will flee seven ways before you this night.

GIDEON. (*Following.*) This night? Is it tonight then, the battle?

THE ANGEL. In panic shall they flee down the Jordan valley. They will try to escape across the Jordan at Beth-barah which is in Ephraim. Therefore, send messengers into Ephraim, and let them say to the chiefs of Ephraim: (*Crosses D. C.*) "Set men at Beth-barah and smite the Midianites as they flee to the fords." Quickly, Gideon, for these are matters of the moment.

GIDEON. (*Coming down defile.*) Sir, these lamps—I cannot flatly march into that tent, saying "Get three hundred lamps and three hundred horns," turn on my heel and flatly walk out again. My captains shall, with some justification, think it a strange instruction.

THE ANGEL. (*Ending all argument.*) I am the Lord. (*Gideon scowls, darts a probing look or two at the Angel, then turns and starts climbing up the defile between the spurs. The Angel sits on bench D. L.*)

JAHLEEL. (*At the tent flap.*) Attend! He comes!

SHILLEM. (*Coming to the tent flap.*) Ho, Gideon! The captains of Asher are here with eight thousand men!

PURAH. (*Whirling and challenging Gideon.*) Who approaches the tent of Gideon?

GIDEON. (*Wearily.*) It is only I, Purah, it is only I.

SHILLEM. (*As Gideon clambers up to the upper spur.*) We have contrived a plan of assault, O General, suggested by Joshua's tactics when he captured the City of Ai. It is our plan to entice the Amalekites off the slopes of Gilboa by sending . . .

HEZEKIAH. Peace be with you, Gideon.

GIDEON. Peace be with you, men of Asher.

SHILLEM. . . . by sending a small band of decoys to the east to . . .

GIDEON. Captains of Asher, gather from your men three hundred lamps, each filled with an hour of oil, and three hundred horns for blowing. (*This gives everybody something to think about for a moment.*)

SHILLEM. Three hundred lamps and three hundred horns. What is the purpose of three hundred lamps and three hundred horns?

GIDEON. You know as much as I. So spoke the Lord to me, and so I speak it to you. (*To Jahleel.*) Captain of Zebulun, send three messengers to the proud prince of Ephraim at Shiloh. Let them say this: "Guard the fords at Bath-barah. This very night, the Midianites, fleeing in panic, will try to cross the Jordan there. Let them smite the Midianites, preserve not one that breathes." Straightaway now, all of you.

MALCHIEL. It is tonight then, that the battle is met?

GIDEON. So spoke the Lord to me.

SHILLEM. Three hundred lamps, each with an hour's oil in it. What are we to do with three hundred lamps?

JAHLEEL. Pray, Gideon, a sensible forethought this guarding the fords at Beth-barah where the Midianites shall flee in panic. What still bears consideration—to me at least—is how does one get the Midianites to flee there in panic?

GIDEON. I am as curious as you. (*He turns on his heel and starts down the defile again.*)

SHILLEM. As gods go, this Lord Yahweh has a whimsical turn of mind, don't you think? Three hundred trumpets. Ha!

MALCHIEL. It is said that with the blowing of trumpets, Joshua took Jericho.

SHILLEM. Well, there was more to it than that, I'm sure. Joshua had a sizeable command of a thousand families.

HEZEKIAH. (*Dubiously.*) I shall go gather the requisitions. (*He exits.*)

SHILLEM. My plan, I thought, had considerable merit. You see, having drawn off the Amalekites . . .

PURAH. (*Whirling to challenge Gideon en route back.*) Who passes there?

GIDEON. Oh, in the name of heaven, you donkey, it is only I!

SHILLEM. Having drawn off the Amalekites, we retire quickly to the east of the Jordan in Gad where we would reassemble the hosts . . .

JAHLEEL. I had better go send messengers to the proud prince of Ephraim. (*He exits,* D. R.)

MALCHIEL. He did not seem especially compelling, this Gideon. We have diviners in Dor whose eyes flash with actual flame. How is this Gideon when prophecy comes upon him? The priests of Cybele leap into the air, slash themselves with knives, spinning and shrieking in Corybantic frenzy till they sink to the ground,

24

self-bloodied eunuchs. The signs have not been good for this battle, Captain of Naphtali. Our men of Acco say a shark washed ashore the day before with a fish in his teeth still wriggling. It is a bad foreboding. (*Gideon has rejoined the Angel* D. L. *He is waiting a little anxiously for the Angel, who is deep in thought, to speak.*)

THE ANGEL. How many men have you in your camp? (*Gideon calculates for a moment.*)

GIDEON. Thirty-two thousand with the eight thousand from Asher.

THE ANGEL. Too many. We shall have to cut your forces down.

GIDEON. (*Unashamedly alarmed.*) Cut them down?

THE ANGEL. If Midian is defeated by thirty-two thousand, then will Israel vaunt itself, saying: "It was by our own hand that we were delivered." And, yea, they shall know it was by the hand of God alone. Now, therefore, go to your chiefs and say: "Proclaim in the ears of the people, saying: 'Whoever is fearful and trembling, let him return home.' "

GIDEON. Oh, dear me!

THE ANGEL. Quickly, Gideon.

GIDEON. (*Crosses* C.) Pray, sir, you have charged me to go to my chiefs and say: "Proclaim in the ears of the people, saying: 'All those who are fearful and trembling, they may return to their farms.' "

THE ANGEL. Aye.

GIDEON. (*Crosses to the Angel.*) Pray, sir, if we were to proclaim in the ears of the people, saying: "All those who are fearful and trembling, you may return to your farms," then, sir, would you see such a sweeping exodus as would make you pale. These hills would be desolate in an hour. And I, in all probability, will be leading the pack. (*Crosses* U. C.)

THE ANGEL. Quickly, Gideon, for we mean to make battle tonight.

GIDEON. This cuirass is unendurable! Why didn't you tell me one wears an undergarment with these things? I had to learn it from Shillem this morning. "Do you not have a sagum underneath?" he said. I didn't even know what a sagum was. He studied me for a moment, unfavorably, to say the least. Oh, sir, surely you must see the consequences—even I who do not know what a sagum is— can see that, if we the fearful of heart to go home, we shall be

25

left with a shocking small army—a few reluctant husbands and some larking boys who think this whole matter a frolic. (*Crosses to the Angel.*) Oh, no, sir, I pray you! Shall I say to my chiefs: "We are outnumbered four to one. Therefore we are too many."? They think me a howling jackal as it is. And they shall think you the same. If you had only seen their faces when I passed on that matter of the oil lamps. (*Crosses* D. C., *sits.*) They looked, to put the kindest word on it, they looked askance at me. Oh, this cuirass!

THE ANGEL. (*Rising into his lordly fury and roaring out.*) I am the Lord! I have said I shall redeem the house of Israel! With one man, if I choose it so, shall I redeem you! (*Gideon looks nervously back to see if they are being overheard. The Angel crosses to Gideon.*) Gideon, take heed! My anger waxes hot against you! I shall consume you with my wrath! I shall open the earth, and I shall swallow you up into the earth.

GIDEON. (*Rather cowed.*) All right, pray, do not shout, sir. All right, it shall be done. (*He turns and with a show of petulance, starts back up the defile. Purah, ever alert fellow, wheels again to challenge him, but Gideon wearily waves him back. As he clambers up to the upper spur, he calls.*) Chiefs of Zebulun, Asher, and Naphtali . . . (*Jahleel, who is back by now, Malchiel, and Shillem rise as Gideon enters the tent.*) Well, harken to this. It is the word of the Lord, spoken in a voice of thunder. You are each to go to his separate camp and proclaim in the ears of your people, saying: "Whoever is fearful and trembling, let him return home."

SHILLEM. Are you insane?

GIDEON. (*His own temper exploding.*) Well, what am I to do? It is the word of the Lord! He spoke it to me; I speak it to you! I too am ill-disposed to this idea! If we are to talk of those who tremble and fear, well, sir, I am surely captain of *that* army! This dreadful cuirass, may it be cursed, and all who put it on them! (*He wrenches at the bindings of the cuirass and takes it off as he storms about.*) If you think you can manage matters better, Naphtalite, well, then, you are general now; I am done with being general! I have been hearing nothing these past two days but what a wily warrior you are. *You* can parley with the Lord. I don't know why he picked on me in the first place!

SHILLEM. Peace, peace, Gideon.

GIDEON. Go and parley with him yourself if you can think you

26

can reap a better crop from him than I! He stands at the foot of that second spur, a large man with a black beard, robed in black linen of such richness as you have never seen. Murmur to him, if you will! Show the stiffness of your neck to him, not to me.

JAHLEEL. But the Lord keeps himself invisible to all but you.

GIDEON. Well, perhaps, I am insane. Have you ever considered that? Not every man who sees a vision is a prophet! You may all be gathered here at the fancy of a maniac! At any moment, I may drop down to all fours and howl like a laboring heifer! (*He wrenches the cuirass off and throws it angrily down.*) Ah! That's better! Look at me, welted and raw. (*Sits on bench.*) And my baldric was on backwards. My manservant shall feel my stick soon enough for that. Well, I shall say once more what was enjoined me by this angel whom only I can see. The Lord Yahweh feels that an army of thirty-two thousand Israelites will detract from the miraculous nature of his deliverance. He wants a smaller army. So go forth to your separate peoples and proclaim in their ears, saying: "Whoever is fearful and trembling, let him return home." (*The Chiefs look questioningly at one another, shrug, and troop out of the tent. Gideon stands wearily for a moment, then goes out of the tent and calls to Purah.*) Purah, go and charge my captains of Manasseh: "Go among the tents of Manasseh and proclaim in the ears of the men, saying: 'All those who fear the battle tonight may go home.'" (*A delighted smile breaks across Purah's face and he leaps to his charge.*) And return here to me. I shall need you. (*Some of his joy abated, Purah exits D. R. It is noticeably darker onstage now. Evening is come. After a moment, the Angel strolls up the defile and goes into the tent.*)

THE ANGEL. Well, they have gone to do as you bid them. You were truly lordly in your wrath.

GIDEON. Thank you.

THE ANGEL. (*Crossing to sit R. of Gideon.*) Now then—by sending the fearful home, you will be left with an army of ten thousand men. And this will still be too many.

GIDEON. I had expected as much.

THE ANGEL. Of these ten thousand who shall be left, three hundred are such great cowards they are even too frightened to escape. You shall know them by the following test: you shall take the ten thousand down to the springs of Harod and let them drink of the water. And those that kneel down to drink, cupping their hands, these shall you send home to their farms. And those that lap the water, as a dog laps, these shall number three hundred. These three hundred, Gideon, shall be your band of deliverers. (*Crosses* u. c.)

GIDEON. For my curiosity alone, why those who lap the water as a dog laps?

THE ANGEL. (*Crossing to Gideon.*) These three hundred are such frightened men they shall lie upon their bellies and lap furtively for fear the Midianites might hear even their drinking.

GIDEON. Well, then, an army of three hundred uncompromising cowards, armed, I assume, with the three hundred oil lamps and the three hundred horns.

THE ANGEL. Ah! You see the battle plan then!

GIDEON. What battle plan?

THE ANGEL. It is an artful ruse. Place one hundred men at Shunem, one hundred more to the north at Endor, and a third company you shall keep right here with you. Then, upon a signal, all three companies shall light their lanterns, wave them in the air, all the while blowing loud blasts on their trumpets. The Midianites will then flee in panic down the valley to Beth-barah where you have already planned a savage greeting for them. (*Gideon regards the Angel for a long moment in a manner that can only be called quizzical.*)

GIDEON. This is the plan for which you had me assemble four tribes of Israel to make war?

THE ANGEL. Aye.

GIDEON. One company of cowards in Shunem, another in Endor, and the third here, waving lanterns and blowing trumpets—that is the substance of it?

THE ANGEL. Aye.

GIDEON. Sir, I have heard at least five plans from that old fraud Shillem that I would deem more probable.

THE ANGEL. Well, it is intended to be a miracle, Gideon.

GIDEON. Oh, that is clear enough. (*He strides out of the tent, throwing up his arms in a gesture of deep annoyance.*) It is a silly plan, sir! A blithe and silly plan! Three hundred tootling cowards will not send a hundred thousand and more men of Midian ranting down the Jordan Valley. The Midianites will simply look up and say: "What is that tootling?" Then they will unsheathe their scimitars, root us out and slash us up. It is a preposterous plan!

28

And see how clear this night! A full moon, not a cloud! No night for hidden warfare, this! That olive bush one mile hence is visible. See! See! The chiefs have told the fearful they can go home. See how they race for their tents. Whisk! That one was folded quickly. And there!, that man is already scuttling down the slope to the caravan road to Bezek. How they scramble! Come and see! (*The Angel ambles out of the tent to join Gideon on the spur.*) How many did you compute would be left? Ten thousand? A rash estimate, my Lord. There will not even be three hundred from which to cull your cowards.

THE ANGEL. Whatever has come over you?

GIDEON. I'm finished with being a soldier.

THE ANGEL. You believed in me this morning.

GIDEON. Yes, then I did, but now I don't.

THE ANGEL. I have given you proofs of my godhood. I have performed wonders at your whim. Yesterday, at this very hour, you tested me. "See," you said, "I place this fleece of wool upon this hill. Now, prove to me you are truly the Lord. In the morning, let me see a heavy dew upon this fleece; but let there be no dew at all on the hill. The hill shall be dry, the fleece alone wet." And I performed this prodigy for you.

GIDEON. Yes, you did.

THE ANGEL. In the morning, it was as you asked. The hill was dry; the fleece was conclusively wet. You seemed convinced. You were effusive in your faith this morning.

GIDEON. Yes, I know. I fell to the ground, didn't I? And shouted: "Turn away from me! Show me not your face! For I have seen the face of the Lord, and I will surely die!" I hope nobody saw us. But then you went off. The sun rose fully up, and the tents around me came awake with the shouts of mortal men. I looked down at the sopping piece of wool in my hand; it seemed a soggy thing to have served a miracle. The fact is, all this dew on the fleece is really not much more than any conjurer's artifice. The diviners of Phrygia are said to change sticks into snakes—I should like to see that. And then I thought: "Well, it's one thing to do sleight-of-hand with pieces of wool but quite another to smite one hundred and twenty thousand Midianites." Oh, well, you know how doubts will gallop. Within an hour, I had arrived at full despair.

THE ANGEL. (*Snorts.*) I too can make sticks into snakes. What

29

manner of snake will you have? An asp? A python? A horned viper? Oh, Gideon, would you have your God a wandering magician, slapping a timbrel and kicking his heels?

GIDEON. Do not rise in wrath against me, sir.

THE ANGEL. (*Crossing* D. L. *in front of ledge.*) I am not in wrath. I am plainly confused. And sore at heart. I have loved you, and and you have turned your back.

GIDEON. (*Crossing to the Angel.*) I do find you personable, sir.

THE ANGEL. (*Turning to Gideon.*) Personable! Gideon, one does not merely fancy God. I demand a splendid love from you, abandoned adoration, a torrent, a storm of love.

GIDEON. (*Crossing away and sitting* C.) I'm afraid I'm not the splendid sort, my Lord.

THE ANGEL. (*Crossing to upper spur.*) I shall make you love me. I'll do another miracle for you, if that will bolster you. The moon is too manifest for you, is it? Shall I eclipse it? Come, tell me what manner of miracle would please you.

GIDEON. No miracles at all. I have no faith in miracles; they are too easily denied. (*He scowls unhappily down at his feet. Then, his face slowly brightens, and he turns to the Angel, bursting with an idea.*) If you could send me a dream, my Lord . . .

THE ANGEL. A dream?

GIDEON. Yes, a dream. I put great stock in dreams.

THE ANGEL. A dream? You will not honor my miracles performed open-handedly before your eyes, but you put great stock in dreams.

GIDEON. (*Crosses* L. *to foot of ledge.*) Oh, sir, it is a well-known fact that dreams portend the future. If I could but have a dream, or, better yet, some other man's. The dreams of other men are frequently more significant.

THE ANGEL. What a devious mind man has developed. Well, then, what would you say to a royal dream? The dream, let us say, dreamed last night by Zalmunna or Zebah, the kings of Midian?

GIDEON. Oh, well, sir, such a dream, of course, would be most portentous. But surely I would not . . .

THE ANGEL. See then, there in that defile, two men, crowned by rubied aigrettes. I really think this must be Zebah and Zalmunna, kings of Midian. Yes, one sees the vivid colors of their tunics now. Royally caparisoned. Oh, that *is* good linen. (*Gideon moves up* to lie on ground beside the Angel. At this point, enter Zebah and Zalmunna, L. They are indeed richly caparisoned. Their jeweled crowns, girdles, sheathes, earrings and pendants glisten and gleam in the moonlight. They are both deeply involved with troubled thoughts.)

ZEBAH. And that is not all. Let us pause here in this quiet spot, for I must tell you of this dream. (They pause at the foot of the spur.)

THE ANGEL. (Sotto voce to Gideon.) What luck! We are going to hear his dream. (Gideon doesn't answer. He has been staring at the kings of Midian in utter amazement, mouth agape and eyes bulging, ever since they were first pointed out to him.)

ZEBAH. (To Zalmunna.) Hear, then, this dream of Zebah, king of Midian. Behold, I dreamed a dream; and lo, a cake of barley bread tumbled into the camp of Midian and came to my tent, and struck it so that it fell, and turned it upside down, so that the tent lay flat. What meaning do you put on this, Zalmunna?

ZALMUNNA. It is an evil dream, Zebah. This is no other than the sword of Gideon the son of Joash, a man of Israel; into his hand God has given Midian and all the host. (Zebah clutches his head with both hands and moans softly. Zalmunna looks nervously around.) Come, let us hurry from this spot. It is frightening here. I hear flappings and flutterings. What are you staring at?

ZEBAH. (So frightened he can hardly talk. He points upward.) The moon! The moon! (Zalmunna looks up, and terror sweeps across his face.)

ZALMUNNA. Eclipsed! It is eclipsed!

ZEBAH. Ay!

ZALMUNNA. (Tugging at his fellow king.) Oh! Come! Come! (He finally tugs Zebah from his petrified fright, and they rush off L. On the upper spur, Gideon, now spotted by the only light on the black stage, stares after the fleeing kings. The expression of astonishment he wore all through this last sudden incident now slowly changes to aghast awe. He stares up at the darkened moon, and then slowly turns to the Angel.)

GIDEON. (Backing slowly away in awe, whispering.) Holy! Holy! Holy! Thou art the Lord! Thou art truly the Lord! (He suddenly cringes, hides his face in his hands.) O! Turn away from me. I have seen the face of the Lord, and I will die!

THE ANGEL. (Moves slowly to Gideon, gently.) Do not fear,

you will not die. I am but a personation of the Lord. (*Gideon sinks to his knees and embraces the knees of the Angel. He slowly lifts his face. His countenance gleams, his lips are parted in a smile of inspirited exaltation. He begins to chant in the fashion of Oriental psalmody.*)

GIDEON.

> Give ear, O Heavens! God our Lord is One!
> Hear, O Kings; give ear, O princes! Glory!
> Proclaim the Name of God, to Him I sing!
> A psalm of love to God, the Lord of Israel!
> I love Thee, Lord.
> Holy! Holy! Holy!

(*The lights dim out slowly.*)

END OF SCENE TWO

"So Gideon and the three companies blew the trumpets
and broke the jars, holding in their left hands the torches,
and in their right hands the trumpets to blow and they
cried . . . 'For the Lord and for Gideon!' "

ACT I

Scene 3

SCENE: *A ridge overlooking the fords at Beth-Barah, some
hours later that night.*

AT RISE: *The Angel is standing patiently stage right,
regarding the battlefield about him. Two Hebrew Soldiers
hurtle in from downstage right.*

FIRST SOLDIER. For the Lord and for Gideon! (*He sounds a
blast on his trumpet and disappears over the ridge. The Second
Soldier pauses to briefly loot one of the bodies on the ground.*)
SECOND SOLDIER. For the Lord and for Gideon! (*He exits
over the ridge. Enter Gideon, running in from* D. L., *panoplied for
war again, sweated and exultant, waving his flambeau and shouting.*)
GIDEON. For the Lord and for Gideon! (*He rushes to the crest of
the ridge where he stands and blows a triumphant blast on his
trumpet.*)
THE ANGEL. Gideon . . .
GIDEON. (*Shouting down into the valley.*) You men of Ephraim,
there by the river! Can you hear me? What is the outcome here?
Have you the kings of Midian, Zebah and Zalmunna, in your
hand?
THE ANGEL. Gideon . . . (*A third soldier dashes in from the
wings and exits over the ridge, shouting.*)
THIRD SOLDIER. For the Lord and for Gideon!
GIDEON. (*Shouting after him.*) Naphtalite! Go to the river bank!
Send me a captain of Ephraim to report the events that have hap-
pened here at Beth-barah!
THE ANGEL. Gideon . . . (*Gideon, at last aware of the Angel,*

33

turns and regards him with shocked and unbelieving eyes, then bursts into exultant laughter.)

GIDEON. My Lord, we won the battle! Were you there at the beginning? Did you see the slaughter that took place in Jezreel? At least thirty thousand Midianites dead in Jezreel alone . . . Carpeted! I say Jezreel is carpeted with Midian's dead! You cannot put your foot down but there is a body underneath it. I say thirty thousand—perhaps more—countless! countless!—and another forty or fifty thousand, trampled, slashed, drowned in their flight down the Jordan Valley to here. It was hideous! Oh, look on this, a child! And that absurd camel there, it makes me cry. (*Indeed he has suddenly begun to cry. The Angel proffers him a leather skin of water and Gideon sits,* C.) Thank you. Oh, I am weary. Picture, if you can, the sleeping camp of Midian at ten o'clock last night. Their tents lay darkly east and west across the Jezreel valley. Some oxen lowed, a clink here and there as the Midianite sentries took up the middle watch. I lit my lamp and shouted: "For the Lord and for Gideon!" On this signal, my three hundred men, now widely spaced in three troops, as you directed, shouted: "For the Lord and for Gideon!", blew trumpets, smashed pottery, stamped their feet and made as much noise as they could. Down below us, the men of Midian came yawning from their tents to see what all the clamor was. Then, suddenly, the cattle in the western camp were in stampede. They came crashing eastward through the tents, raising up a storm of dust so that no man knew his brother. The Midianites in the east, thinking themselves besieged, leaped into the dust with their swords, and the Midianites of the west, fleeing before their cattle, found themselves engaged in war with their own brothers, until, my Lord, the whole vast multitude, one hundred thousand men and women, their young and old and all their animals, fled in shrieking frenzy to the Jordan River. I stood upon the hill at Harod, transfixed by the sight of it! (*A Fourth Soldier enters, shouting.*)

FOURTH SOLDIER. For the Lord and for Gideon! (*Exits.*)

GIDEON. (*Crossing* U. C.) Then, at the Jordan, down from the hills came the men of Naphtali and Asher and the houses of Manasseh with their sickles and plowshares and reaped the Midianites as so much wheat. At last, the shreds and tatters of this mighty host came splashing into the shoals here at Beth-barah where the men of Ephraim sprang from their ambush and smote the survivors until surely there is not one left that breathes. The vultures will be flapping thick tomorrow. I see the soldiers have begun to gather the stray cows and sheep. There is much looting going on. Indeed, I stripped a corpse myself just before. (*He indicates a jeweled sheathe on his baldric, and tries to pull out the falcate sword from the sheath, he can't get it out.*) They have a strange curved sword, these Midianites, with the honed edge outward. One slashes away. (*He crosses to the Angel and falls at his feet.*) It seems awkward. Oh, my Lord, it came to pass, as you said. One hundred and twenty thousand Midianites lie slain this night. How great you are, my Lord, and how impermanent is man. (*He begins to snicker and giggle.*) Forgive me, my Lord, forgive me . . . (*In a moment, he has yielded to a spasm of uncontrollable laughter. He stands, clutching his sides, shouting and wheezing, lurching about, stumbling over bodies. He manages to squeeze out bursts of sentences.*) Oh, my Lord! You will not believe this! Oh! It is so comical, let me gather my wits! Oh, I am a foolish ass indeed! Oh! Oh! Oh! My Lord, one hunderd twenty thousand Midianites were slain this night, the entire host of them, or so it seems! Oh! Oh! One hundred twenty thousand of them slain, and I, the captain of the hosts of Israel—Oh! Oh! Oh!—and I, my Lord, I, the captain of the hosts, did not so much as unsheathe my dagger! I took no part at all in the whole bloody battle! Do you understand, my Lord? Oh! I never got within a mile of a Midianite! I watched the whole night from the hills! (*It is too much for him. Gideon has to lie down flat on his back. Tears of laughter stream from his eyes. After a moment, he sits up, spent and sighing.*) Forgive me, my Lord. I have been shaken badly this night. I am not my own master.

THE ANGEL. It is not yet finished, Gideon. The kings of Midian with fifteen thousand of their men have escaped across the river.

GIDEON. Oh? I shall have to gather my three hundred men. (*Wearily, starts to rise.*)

THE ANGEL. No, no, rest, Gideon. There are some moments yet till dawn. You shall pursue after Zebah and Zalmunna then.

GIDEON. (*Lying back exhausted on the ground.*) The kings of Midian . . .

THE ANGEL. (*Crossing U. C.*) The kings of Midian are half-way to the walled city of Karkor. You will have them in your hand tomorrow night. Now rest and spend this interlude with me. (*Crosses* D. R. C., *next to Gideon.*)

GIDEON. (*Closing his eyes.*) Have I found favor in your eyes tonight, my Lord?

THE ANGEL. (*Gently.*) Indeed you have. (*The Angel now sits cross-legged beside Gideon's resting body. A silence falls between the two.*)

GIDEON. (*After a moment.*) Have you loved many men, my Lord?

THE ANGEL. I love all men It is my essence.

GIDEON. I mean, men with whom you have truly commerced face-to-face as you have with me.

THE ANGEL. Five or six, perhaps.

GIDEON. Were they as pleasing to you as I am, my Lord?

THE ANGEL. (*Smiling.*) What a vain fellow you are.

GIDEON. Understand, my Lord, I do not hold these other loves to your discredit.

THE ANGEL. Are you being kind to me, Gideon? Now you must own that is vain of you. And you are something of a prig too, taking this high moral tone, even if I were no more than the dissolute lady you seem to think me.

GIDEON. Oh, my Lord, you are God, and your name is One!

THE ANGEL. I am just teasing you, Gideon.

GIDEON. I love you more than I have ever loved anyone.

THE ANGEL. I know you do.

GIDEON. I thought of nothing but you the whole night. I am possessed by all the lunacy of love. If I could, I would cover you with veils, God, and keep you hidden behind the curtains in my tent. Oh! Just say again you love me, God.

THE ANGEL. I do, Gideon.

GIDEON. I do not know why. I must say, I do not know why.

THE ANGEL. I hardly know why myself, but then passion is an unreasonable thing. (*He leans back against a rock, rather pensive.*) Let me consider. I have loved five men, or six if I add in Phinehas, but I could not say I truly loved Phinehas. Phinehas was high-priest in the years that followed Joshua, and we spoke ten times or so of sacerdotal things, the setting of the year's calendar, such matters as that. A nice man, Phinehas, good family, son of Eleazar the son of Aaron—you cannot be better bred than that; but, still, not my sort. Too pinch-penny with his passions. The costive soul

36

makes priests; it does not make lovers. Abraham, Isaac, Jacob of course,—Joshua. But the man I most loved was Moses.

GIDEON. Yes?

THE ANGEL. I loved him very much I do not think I shall love any man so much again. And he was scarcely Hebrew. He was bred as an Egyptian and married a gentile woman. Yes, I think the man was still uncircumcised the day I first beheld him herding sheep at Horeb, a hulking, hare-lipped, solitary man, quite unattractive really, stammered, dour—nay, say sullen—lacking wit, one of those ever-earnest fellows. Yet I fancied Moses from the very first. Gaunt he stood against the crags of Horeb, a monumentally impassioned man. It is passion, Gideon, that carries man to God. And passion is a balky beast. Few men ever let it out the stable. It brooks no bridle; indeed, it bridles you; it rides the rider. Yet, it inspirits man's sessile soul above his own inadequate world and makes real such things as beauty, fancy, love, and God and all those other things that are not quite molecular but are. Passion is the very fact of God in man that makes him other than a brute. I must own, Gideon, yours was an old and cold and settled soul, and I huffed and puffed quite a bit before I found the least flame of passion in you.

GIDEON. What is it that you love in me, my Lord? These other men were saints or prophets, but I am an ordinary sort. I am as all men are.

THE ANGEL. Well, perhaps *that* is your special attraction, your ordinariness. I would have plain men love me, not just saints.

GIDEON. Well, that isn't very nice.

THE ANGEL. Oh, Gideon, you are difficult.

GIDEON. Well, I do not think it gratifying to be loved for one's lack of distinction. (*He stands, ruffled. Crosses* R.) I thought I managed my duties well tonight.

THE ANGEL. Indeed, you did.

GIDEON. To speak plainly, I think I make a good show of being general. I have a commanding voice and am not unhandsome in my armor.

THE ANGEL. You make a splendid figure.

GIDEON. You find me amusing.

THE ANGEL. Well, you are a pompous ass.

GIDEON. (*Crosses to the Angel and kneels.*) Yes, so I am. (*His natural good humor returns, and he laughs agreeably at himself.*)

37

Oh, it is indeed the truth, God. Like all modest men, I am impossibly vain. I amuse even myself, strutting about, shouting—well, not really shouting; I'm cleverer than that at the charade. I put myself forth more as the calm but resolute general, imperative but not forbidding. What a peacock I am! It is amusing, isn't it?

THE ANGEL. It is. (*Gideon sits down beside the Angel, a little sad now.*)

GIDEON. I have had very little esteem in my life, my Lord, and I do not think there is much harm in my relishing this one moment of honor. I have this one son, Jether, who is twelve years old, the son of my first wife, and even he uses me lightly. I am not esteemed, my Lord, even in my own tent, and this has given me great pain. (*The Angel regards Gideon compassionately.*)

THE ANGEL. I shall give you seventy sons, Gideon; they shall praise your name. You shall know the ardor of many wives.

GIDEON. I should like that.

THE ANGEL. Oh, Gideon, I shall bless you. I shall make your fields to prosper. I shall make your cattle fat. Your father shall kneel before you and embrace your knees. All Israel shall say: "Regard Gideon; he is the most blessed of men, for he is beloved of God." You seem displeased by all this good fortune. (*This last in reference to a scowl deepening on Gideon's brow and the fact that he has stood up.*)

GIDEON. Yes, well, all this greatness, all this good fortune which you will make mine, will not really be mine. It is all but a gift from God. There is no honor that reflects to me in it at all, merely that I am beloved of God.

THE ANGEL. Well, that is a somewhat less than gracious thing to say. The love of God will not suffice for you indeed.

GIDEON. (*Ashamed.*) I spoke coarsely, Lord. Forgive me.

THE ANGEL. I wonder if this vanity of yours is as ingenuous as it seemed, and if it is not a sinister thing rather. What is vanity in man really, but the illusion that he has a purpose? Do not presume to matter, Gideon, for in the house of God you matter not. My universe is large beyond your knowing; there is no beginning, there is no end to it. You are a meaningless thing and live only in my eye. I shall make you great, Gideon, because I love you; but it is merely my caprice. If you displease me, I shall destroy you in a whim of temper. To love me, Gideon, you must abandon all your vanities. They are presumptuous and will come between us.

GIDEON. (*Truly penitent.*) Oh, my Lord, that could never be.

THE ANGEL. Consider how you have already reduced me to some kind of clever if wanton lady who finds you handsome and sends you into battle with her handkerchief.

GIDEON. My Lord, I . . .

THE ANGEL. Surely, I shall see you tomorrow vaunting yourself before the armies, saying it was by your hand, and not mine, that Israel was redeemed from the Midianites.

GIDEON. Oh, my Lord, I would sooner cut my throat with this— (*He wrenches at his Midianite sword again, and again it sticks to its scabbard.*) —with this— Oh! How do they manage with these things? At any rate, if I could get it out of its scabbard, I would slit my throat with it before I derogated you, my Lord.

THE ANGEL. (*Laughing.*) Oh, Gideon. I love you, and I will exalt you over all men. But I fear you will betray me. (*Gideon gives up on the sword, turns to the Angel and regards him with manifest devotion. He kneels before the Angel, takes the latter's hand and presses it to his lips.*)

GIDEON. (*Fervently.*) The Lord is my God, the Lord is One. He is vast, ineffable, the maker and the mover of all things, and He has paused to love me; shall I ask for other blessings? God, do not fear my vanity. I will never betray you. (*The Angel, touched, gently strokes the bowed head before him. Enter tired Soldiers, straggling slowly across the stage.*)

SOLDIER. (*Wearily.*) For the Lord and for Gideon. (*They disappear over the ridge. The first streaks of dawn are now lightening the sky. The Angel marks the coming of day.*)

THE ANGEL. It's morning now, Gideon. (*He is interrupted by the entrance of Shillem. That is, two Soldiers enter, bracing a rubber-legged and wheezing Shillem between them. Despite his dreadful condition, the old man holds fast to his warbow. The Angel notes Shillem's entrance with a smile.*) The troops of Shillem have come.

SHILLEM. (*Gasping away, to the two Soldiers.*) Here—set me here. (*The two Soldiers sit him gently down, propped up against a large rock where he slumps, all but dead of exhaustion.*)

GIDEON. Oh, Shillem! I told you to stay behind. You will exhaust yourself with all this racing up and down these hills. (*To the Angel.*) The old popinjay fell in a faint five minutes after the slaughter in Jezreel began. It seems the sight of blood sickens him.

39

THE ANGEL. (*Laughing.*) Go then, Gideon, and find Shethulah, the prince of Ephraim. He's very arrogant and will not like a man from Manasseh such as you ordering him about.

GIDEON. Oh, dear. (*To the two Soldiers* L. C.) Go and join your fellows on the river bank. I will be shortly there. (*The two Soldiers exit.*)

THE ANGEL. (*To Gideon.*) The spirit of the Lord shall be with you. (*He exits* D. L., *with a casual wave of his hand.*)

GIDEON. (*Giving Shillem his skin of water.*) Here, drink this and rest. (*It is more than Shillem can manage to even raise the skin of water to his lips. It dangles slackly from his fingers.*)

SHILLEM. Oh, Gideon, tell no one, I beg you, that I swooned at the sight of battle.

GIDEON. Shillem, my old captain, we are all wretched cowards, the full three hundred of us.

SHILLEM. I spent the night, hiding in a cave, clutching my war-bow.

GIDEON. Yes, I know. Now, rest here. I must go find the proud prince of Ephraim and learn the state of things here at Beth-barah. (*He exits over the ridge. Shillem, alone now, allows himself a sob or two.*)

SHILLEM. Oh, how despicable I am. Let all men know that Shillem is a coward, a rabbit, a . . . (*He breaks off as Hezekiah and Malchiel and two soldiers enter from* R., *waving their lamps and shouting:*)

HEZEKIAH, MALCHIEL, SOLDIERS. For the Lord and for Gideon! (*They are about to clamber across the ridge when Hezekiah sees Shillem sprawled* D. *Hezekiah comes puffing down to the old man, sits beside him, crosses his legs, sighs, and says:*)

HEZEKIAH. Well, we seem to have won the war and decimated the entire host of Midian—how did we ever manage to do that? Well, I daresay we shall find sensible explanations for everything. You were with Gideon, were you not? That put you in the thick of it. Did you kill many of the enemy? (*A brief struggle for virtue ensues in Shillem.*)

SHILLEM. (*Mumbling.*) Two or three.

HEZEKIAH. Two or three, did you say?

SHILLEM. Dozen.

HEZEKIAH. Two or three dozen!

SHILLEM. Yes, I was with Gideon, as you say, when the Midianite

40

herds broke into stampede. Seeing the Midianites disconcerted, I led a charge down from my hill, panicking the foe into headlong flight to the Jordan valley. This, I would have to say, was the pivotal point of the battle. (*Malchiel, who has been walking slowly about the stage, examining the battlefield, now looks up, his bold, fanatic eyes blazing in his dark, sweated face.*)

MALCHIEL. We have heard fantastic stories of Gideon's deeds. A woman of Manasseh told us she saw Gideon leap from a tree into a pack of ten Midianites and smite them all with ten strokes of his spear.

SHILLEM. She told you all wrong. His weapon was an ox-goad, and there were twenty of the foe, not ten.

HEZEKIAH. Twenty?

MALCHIEL. Twenty men did Gideon smite with an ox-goad! Here, look on this! A serpent has coiled itself upon this fallen Midianite. This augurs significantly.

HEZEKIAH. (*Nudging Shillem.*) My brother is adroit at divination.

MALCHIEL. (*With fanatic fervor.*) What manner of god is this Yahweh of Gideon's? His incarnation is the bull; his ideogram is the coiled serpent. (*He scoops up a handful of dirt and lets it fall back to the ground. He kneels and studies the patterns it makes.*)

HEZEKIAH. (*Winking at Shillem.*) My brother divines from the configurations of the ground and sees great significance in pebbles.

MALCHIEL. (*Studying the geomantic pattern.*) Regard. A crescent moon and, here again!, a coiled viper upon a cloven heart. O, dazzling among gods is this Yahweh; he is both sun and moon; and Gideon is his only son. Behold! The morning star! Gideon is single among men as the morning star is single in the heavens! Sing praise! Cry out for Gideon! The son of Yahweh, the bull-god! Ay! (*He stands stiffly upright and promptly falls into a dead faint. Shillem, rather taken aback by this, sits up with a start.*)

HEZEKIAH. He'll be all right. He is given to these ecstatic moments.

SHILLEM. Is he really?

HEZEKIAH. He spends much time with Phoenician priests who are emotional. But I prefer to find more reasonable explanations for things than gods. I am not a little known in my own city of Kanah as a scholar and have predicted several eclipses. I read and write a competent Egyptian hand and have some knowledge of medicinal herbs. Actually, I attracted some attention in learned circles a few years ago with my theory of the ecliptic of the sun; you may have heard something of that.

SHILLEM. Look here, are we to leave your brother lying around like that?

HEZEKIAH. I think that when all the facts are known, this improbable battle will seem more probable. It was a clever stratagem of Gideon's, stampeding the cattle, and, of course, your opportune assault on the Midianite flank explains much of the enemy's panic. Piece by piece, the events of the night become less mystical.

SHILLEM. On my soul! (*This last refers to the entrance of Shethulah, a prince of Ephraim, followed by several soldiers, who loom up from the u. side of the ridge. Shethulah is holding aloft two grisly decapitated heads.*)

SHETHULAH. Behold the heads of Oreb and Zeeb, princes of Midian, the sons of the kings of Midian. (*Malchiel remains in his trance. Hezekiah rises.*) Which of you three is Gideon the son of Joash the Abiezrite?

SHILLEM. He has gone to the river to find the prince of Ephraim.

SHETHULAH. I am the prince of princes of Ephraim. I am Shethulah the son of Elishama, the son of Ammihud, the son of Ephraim, the son of Joseph. Bring forth this Gideon, send men after him so that he may account to me for what he did, that he has made war on Midian but he did not ask my counsel? Is not Ephraim the prince among all the tribes of Israel, the most populous in number, the richest in wealth? Who shall lead the tribes of Israel in war? Shall it not be Ephraim? (*Hezekiah considers this statement with scholarly detachment.*)

HEZEKIAH. (*To Shillem.*) These Ephraimites are so superior really. There's no historical basis for it at all, you know.

SHETHULAH. (*Crosses* D. R.) Captain of Asher, go with your men down to the valley and chop off the hands of all the dead that we may make a count of how many slain.

HEZEKIAH. Sir, it's all very well to play the proud prince with the chief of Naphtali here and me, but I suggest you be more humble when Gideon comes. Know the manner of man this Gideon is. Know that Gideon leaped from a tree and smote— (*Turns to Shillem.*) How many did you say, twenty?

SHILLEM. Did I say twenty? Oh, well, in that case, it was nearer

42

forty. (*For a long moment, Hezekiah studies Shillem with the scientist's skeptical eye. Then, he turns back to Shethulah.*)

HEZEKIAH. Eighty men did Gideon smite with an ox-goad.

SHETHULAH. (*Very impressed.*) Eighty men! (*At this moment, Malchiel springs up to his feet with a shrill cry.*)

MALCHIEL. Ay! The vision of Malchiel! The oracle of a man whose eye is opened! Hear the history of Gideon.

SHILLEM. (*Crying out.*) Tell us your vision, oh, holy man!

HEZEKIAH. (*Seizing the elbow of the startled Shethulah.*) My brother, sir, is adroit at divination and not to be taken lightly. (*Gideon appears, coming up from the far side of the ridge. He pauses on the crest, to hear Malchiel's testimony. At the same time, the Angel enters and stands* D. R., *watching.*)

MALCHIEL. (*In a trance.*) The great god, Yahweh, the god of Moses, who is the bull, who is the lion; in his left hand is a crescent sword, in his right hand is a ball of fire; he saw a woman of Manasseh. He leaned over her lips. He raised his voice and said: "Behold her lips are as sweet as a bunch of grapes." In the perfume of the cedars did they lay. When dawn broke, a cloud black as night rose from heaven's foundations. The great god Yahweh rose into the sky in a chariot of lapis-lazuli and gold. In the arms of the Manassehite woman he placed an infant. On its brow was coiled the sacred asp. Behold! It was Gideon, the man-god, the son of Yahweh, the redeemer of Israel, the man of valor, the god Gideon! (*A silence follows this enthusiastic statement.*)

GIDEON. (*From the crest of the ridge.*) Oh, Malchiel, you cannot be serious. (*All whirl at the sound of Gideon's voice. Malchiel falls to his knees and prostrates himself.*)

SHILLEM. There, ye Ephraimites, stands Gideon, who with an ox-goad smote one hundred men! (*Gideon bursts into laughter.*)

GIDEON. A hundred men! Oh, Shillem, what a fearful fiction! What have you been telling this noble man? For you, sir, must surely be Shethulah, the prince of princes in Ephraim. (*He descends in obsequious haste from the ridge. For a moment He and Shethulah, who is now in abject awe of Gideon, vie with each other in the gestures of deference.*)

SHETHULAH. (*Humbly proffering the decapitated heads of the Midianite princes to Gideon.*) Behold the heads of Oreb and Zeeb, the princes of Midian.

GIDEON. (*Crossing to the Angel.*) Don't give them to me. I wouldn't know what to do with them. Hang them on the walls of your city. I think that is the practice. (*Winking at the Angel.*) How many did he have me killing with an ox-goad, one hundred? (*He bursts into laughter, to Shethulah.*) The truth is, great lord, I killed no Midianites at all. (*Shethulah looks up startled.*)

SHETHULAH. You killed no Midianites at all.

GIDEON. (*Beaming.*) Not a one. (*Rage sweeps across the Ephraimite prince's face. He is furious at being gulled and regards Shillem and Hezekiah with a fierce eye.*)

SHETHULAH. Then, Gideon, you shall account to me for what you have done, that you made war against Midian and did not seek my counsel. Shall Manasseh lead the hosts and Ephraim be the scavengers? Did not Jacob bless Ephraim before his brother, saying: "Ephraim shall be greater than his brother Manasseh"? I shall take command of the hosts of Israel now, Gideon! (*He seizes a whip from one of the soldiers and would lash Gideon but is intercepted by Gideon.*)

GIDEON. Hear, O Ephraimite! Do not contend with me for glory, for it is neither yours nor is it mine! This glory is the Lord's! Give praise to the Lord! for he has triumphed gloriously. Bow down! (*All sink to their knees and bow their heads down to the ground. Gideon surveys the supplicating backs for a moment, then turns and slowly walks to where the Angel stands* R., *regarding Gideon with effulgent love, Gideon prostrates himself before the Angel.*) Did you truly fear my vanity? O, timeless and immane God, I yearn after you and seek only to be pleasing in your eye.

THE ANGEL. Rise up, good Gideon, and pursue after the kings of the enemy. (*Gideon stands.*)

GIDEON. Rise up! We have more war to make! These are my charges to you all. Let the Ephraimites count the dead and bury them that the land may be clean of carrion and that the jackals may not overrun us. Captains of Asher and Naphtali, come with me. We shall pursue after the kings of Midian. (*The others all stand. Again, Gideon tries to wrench his Midianite sword from its scabbard to flourish it, but again it sticks in its sheathe. Flourishing his empty hand instead, He shouts:*) For Gideon and for the Lord! (*He leaps out of view over the ridge. Shillem,*

Hezekiah, Malchiel and soldiers, brandishing their weapons, exit quickly after him.)

SHILLEM, HEZEKIAH, MALCHIEL and SOLDIERS. For Gideon and for the Lord! *(The Ephraimites follow after them, more slowly and with less enthusiasm, but nevertheless shouting.)*

THE EPHRAIMITES. For Gideon and for the Lord! *(They exit over the ridge. The Angel is now left alone onstage, frowning thoughtfully. He detaches himself from the arch and shuffles to C. where He tugs at his beard pensively.)*

THE ANGEL. *(Muttering.)* For Gideon and for the Lord, indeed. It used to be: "For the Lord and for Gideon." *(He shrugs in the ageless Hebrew fashion and strides off L. The curtain comes down quickly.)*

END OF ACT ONE

"And the elders of Succoth said, Are Zebah and Zalmunna in your hand, that we should give bread to your
army? And Gideon said, Therefore when the Lord has
delivered Zebah and Zalmunna into my hand, then I
will tear your flesh."

ACT II

SCENE 1

A threshing floor on a hill by the city of Succoth.
The time is two days later in the afternoon.
AT RISE: *There are three senior gentlemen, obviously*
prisoners, standing disconsolately stage L. A rope joins
their necks, and their hands are tied in front of them.
These are the Elders of Succoth. There are seventy-four
more of them offstage. We can perhaps see one or two.
A guard stands in attendance on them.
A second soldier stares off upstage over a parapet. He is
apparently a lookout.
The Angel now appears climbing up to the top of the
threshing floor. He stands a moment, amiably looking
around.
Suddenly the lookout straightens to attention and shouts:

THE LOOKOUT. Gideon is here! He is at the gates!
VOICE. (*Off.*) He comes! Gideon comes! (*Shouts and alarum*
off, Shillem suddenly looms up out of the pit, clambering up the
threshing floor.)
SHILLEM. Prepare the feast! Soldiers, clear the space before the
gates! Maidens, bring fruit here, bring wine! Bring skewers of
meat for Gideon! (*More shouts and alarum off down in the pit.*

46

Maidens come scurrying up bearing bowls of pomegranates, grapes, figs, slabs of steaming mutton, and skins of wine. Shethulah, the Ephraimite prince, also enters, champing away on a leg of lamb as he does. Both he and Shillem are nicely drunk. Shillem regards the elders standing L.) The elders of Succoth, are they all here? Seven and seventy of them? Oh, you wretched chiefs of Succoth! You will surely die today. This is what Gideon charged me this morning: "Go in advance, Shillem," said he, "my mighty captain, and capture the seven and seventy elders of Succoth, for they are Hebrews; yet, they jeered at the word of the Lord. The wrath of God is hot against them and they shall die." *(A ram's horn is heard far offstage. Shouting down into the pit.)* Bugler, sound your trumpet! *(The ram's horn sounds offstage, closer than before, and the Bugler onstage responds. The stage crowds up with people.)*

ALL. *(Singing.)*
> Hosanna! Hosanna!
> Make melody to Gideon!
> Barak has slain his thousands!
> But Gideon tens of thousands!
> He is as the wild ox who gores the foe!
> Barak has slain his thousands!
> But Gideon tens of thousands!
> O Israel! O Israel!
> Israel! Israel!

VOICES. They are here! They are here! Gideon is here! *(Indeed, Malchiel comes bouncing up to the top of the threshing floor where He stands addressing the multitude in the pit.)*

MALCHIEL. We have won the battle of Karkor! With twenty thousand men of Reuben and Gad, we smote the last of Midian! There is not one left that breathes! Great was the glory of Barak, of Ehud and Othniel, but sovereign is the glory of Gideon. Bow down! *(Everyone on the threshing floor and presumably everyone in the pit bends low in homage. A hush falls on the stage. In the midst of it, Gideon enters climbing up from the pit, followed by Hezekiah and two women who thrust baskets of grapes and pomegranates at the conquering hero.)*

FIRST WOMAN. The first grapes of the year, my lord Gideon.

SECOND WOMAN. The first of the summer fruits, my lord Gideon. *(Gideon seems pleased by all this homage. He surveys*

47

the pit below him rather grandly. The Angel now crosses to Gideon and claps him heartily on the back. Gideon turns startled. A quick look of apprehension sweeps over his face. He wheels on the obeisant people around him and below him and thunders out.)

GIDEON. Be still, you foolish people! Am I the Lord that you bring me first fruits? Make no god of me! It was the Lord that redeemed you from Midian! Rise up, then, rise up! *(He looks for approval from the Angel and almost stumbles over a maiden at his feet. She is a darkly savage and sinuous thing of fourteen, a marriageable age in those days.)* Rise up, you silly woman. Whose maiden is this?

SHILLEM. She is Orpah the daughter of the elder Ozni, standing there.

GIDEON. The daughter of Ozni? He was most guilty of all the elders. Poor maiden, her father shall die first. *(Turns to the elders, raising a foreboding finger at them.)* Regard the elders of Succoth!

OZNI. *(An Elder, flinging himself at Gideon's feet.)* O, Puissant Gideon!, hear our suffrage.

A SECOND ELDER. Pity us, my lord.

A THIRD ELDER. O, pity us, sire.

GIDEON. One day ago, you elders, my three hundred men and I, hot in pursuit of Zebah and Zalmunna, came to these gates. And you seven and seventy elders of Succoth with Ozni the son of Deuel at your head came forth to meet us. "Pray," I said, "give loaves of bread to the people who follow me; for they are faint, and I am pursuing after Zebah and Zalmunna, the kings of Midian." And you all did taunt me. "Are Zebah and Zalmunna already in your hand," you said to me, "that we should give bread to your army?" "These are the soldiers of the Lord!" I said. "Give them food, or will you mock the Lord?" And you, Ozni, son of Deuel, then said: "Show us Zebah and Zalmunna in your hand, and we shall give you loaves of bread." Well, then, bring forth Zebah and Zalmunna! *(Enter Zebah and Zalmunna, their hands tied in front of them, their necks joined by a rope. They are guarded by two soldiers.)* Behold! Zebah and Zalmunna, the kings of Midian, are in my hand! *(The two kings drop to their knees, place their faces at Gideon's feet. Gideon puts a foot on the neck of Zebah.)* We do not practice mutilation in Israel. I shall kill you plainly, Zebah and Zalmunna. *(With a quick, strong, downward thrust, Gideon plunges his spear into Zebah's ribs. The Midianite king emits a short, strangled gasp and topples over dead. The spear remains in Gideon's hand, now dripping red with blood. With a second quick thrust, he dispatches Zalmunna who screams out shrilly and falls, the spear protruding slantwise from under his arm. A frightened silence fills the stage.)* This was Midian, a violent tribe. They lived ten generations. They are no more. As it was with the kings of Midian, O elders, so shall it be with you. *(Gideon wrenches the spear loose from Zalmunna's body, turns, strides to the Elders on the tower, raising his spear above his head.)* The Voice of the Lord came to me, thundering: "Smite the elders of Succoth, preserve not one, so that all Israel may know the fear of God!" *(But the sheer piteousness of the three old men before him stays his hand. Mutely, they stare up at him, tears streaming down their cheeks. One of the Maidens breaks into a high-pitched wail. Gideon lowers his spear, darts a nervous look at the Angel.)* Well, I'm faint; I marched all day. Set food and wine before me that I may eat and drink. I shall kill these old men after that. *(The Maidens scurry off. Gideon addresses the host of people onstage.)* Give praise to the Lord, for he is the kinsman, he is the rock, he is a man of war. Bow down! *(The people all go down upon their knees and bow their heads forward so that their brows touch the floor between their hands—the full salaam. Gideon regards the stage of bowed backs, then turns and looks for the Angel, now at D. R. Gideon ambles over, rubbing his neck and sighing wearily.)* I slept two hours last night, if that much, and ache in every bone. We left Karkor at break of day. It is almost thirty miles and a mountainous route. I had not thought to see you here, my Lord.

THE ANGEL. Will you not embrace me?

GIDEON. Oh, indeed, yes, of course. *(He kneels quickly, kisses the hem of the Angel's robe, and stands.)*

THE ANGEL. That was perfunctory, Gideon.

GIDEON. Well, I made battle all last night, God, and marched all day and ate nothing but some figs and cake. I do not feel affectionate at the moment.

THE ANGEL. You are not pleased that I am here.

GIDEON. Well, I have many things to do, my Lord. *(Crosses C.)* It would be better if you waited for me at my tent at Ophrah.

THE ANGEL. Like your other wives.

GIDEON. You are being quarrelsome. You know you are more than wife to me. I am on edge and close to temper, and I pray you, leave me to myself for the moment.

THE ANGEL. As you say. I shall wait beside your tent at Ophrah for you.

GIDEON. I should be home within a day or two.

THE ANGEL. Will you not embrace me before I go? (*Gideon sighs a brief sigh of exasperation, goes to his knees again, and brushes the hem of the Angel's robe with his lips. The Angel starts off, but Gideon, still on his knees, calls him.*)

GIDEON. Oh, my Lord?

THE ANGEL. (*Turning.*) Yes.

GIDEON. (*Standing.*) My Lord, about these elders of Succoth here. You came to me in a dream last night and said: "Smite them all, preserve not one that breathes." Yet, I wonder, is that not perhaps too harsh a penalty? They seem so piteous a lot of senior gentlemen. And they are Hebrews, my Lord. They are our people.

THE ANGEL. They made light of the Lord. Will you pass by while men make light of me?

GIDEON. I thought perhaps to scourge them with whips, forty lashes less one for each. That would surely instruct them in the fear of God.

THE ANGEL. (*Indicating the elders.*) These men are utter wretches, Gideon. Of all the clans of Gad, these men of Succoth have done most evilly in mine eyes. I have had it in mind several times to strike them down.

GIDEON. I pity them, my Lord.

THE ANGEL. It is not just this matter of their taunting you. The men of Succoth have married their sons to the daughters of Moab and practice the ways of Moab. They lie with men as with a woman and uncover the nakedness of their own daughters. They eat unslaughtered meat with its carrion blood still in it, oppress the stranger and revile the widow and the orphan. They are a miscreant folk. Smite these elders, every one, Gideon, preserve not one, so that all Israel may hear and fear, so that the name of the Lord shall be a name of terror in their hearts, and they shall walk in my ways again.

GIDEON. Well, I shall kill them then since you wish it.

50

THE ANGEL. (*Crosses to Gideon.*) Oh, Gideon, you make so much of death. You must not be so temporal. It is all right for the bulk of men to fear death, for in death they fear me. But, in truth, there isn't anything to it at all. Nothing happens, nothing changes; the essence of things goes on. You see, you measure things in time, but there is no time in truth. You live now ten million years ago and are at this moment ten million years hence, or more; for there are no years. The slaying of seventy-seven elders happens but it does not happen, for they live even so and have died before, and all is now, which was and is forever. Oh, dear, I see this is heavy going for you.

GIDEON. Well, I follow you here and there a bit; not everything of course.

THE ANGEL. Well, you shouldn't bother your head with all these speculations anyway. I am the final truth of all things, Gideon, so you need only love me and live your life as I will it for you, and it shall be a seemly thing.

GIDEON. My point, you see, is that I pity these old men.

THE ANGEL. Of course you do. But you are being vain again, for to pity a man's death is to say his life was significant, which it isn't. Now, let us have an end to this. Go and smite the elders. I am the Lord.

GIDEON. As you say.

THE ANGEL. (*Turning to go.*) Then, peace be with you, Gideon. I shall wait for you beside your tent.

GIDEON. (*Nervously shuffling his feet.*) My Lord—

THE ANGEL. Yes?

GIDEON. My Lord—oh, how shall I say it? My Lord, the people have made much of me these past few days. Well, as you see, even here in Succoth. But what an ovation was accorded to me at Mahanaim! Great crowds gathered along the highway and shouted my name. Maidens came forth with dancing and with timbrels. I fancy that sort of thing, as, of course, you know. And twice today, Malchiel there, who is an enthusiastic man, stood up before thousands—at Mahanaim and at Jogbehah too— and called me king, and the people shouted as with one voice: "Amen!" I would like to be king, my Lord.

THE ANGEL. But Gideon—

GIDEON. I could hardly sleep last night for thinking of myself as king. That demon vanity crept into my tent like a succubus

51

and had me trying on different crowns, diadems from Babylon and pschents from Egypt. I finally dropped off, having decided I looked best with no crown at all, a modest king, receiving the ambassadors from Armenia while plowing his own fields, distinguishable from his servants only by his noble bearing. Well, you know what a vain ass I am. O, Lord, could I not be king of Israel?

THE ANGEL. Gideon, I am king of Israel. To say Israel needs another king suggests I am inadequate.

GIDEON. (*In a burst of temper.*) I do not think I ask so very much! I do not say I will usurp your throne. I only ask for a nominal crown and a few trappings. Some purfled robes, perhaps a modest palace. You are ever accusing me of wishing to cheat you! Indeed, I meant to make your name greater. I would build altars for you and enforce your laws. All I asked was a bit of pomp because I am a vain fellow and like to preen before the people. Well, then I am vain! That is my manner! You could indulge me in this minor frailty. Just this one time!

THE ANGEL. (*At first startled, now furious.*) Do you shout at the Lord?

GIDEON. (*Striding angrily about.*) I have served you well, have I not? You vowed you would exalt me above my fellows. And do not say you did not, because you did. You said you would bless me and that you would do such and such, and, in particular, you said you would exalt me above my fellows.

THE ANGEL. Gideon, beware!

GIDEON. (*Turning sulkily away.*) I warned you I was in a temper.

THE ANGEL. You are a presumptuous man!

GIDEON. (*Sitting D. C.*) Nor is it an easy thing to love you, God.

THE LORD. I struck Korah down, and all his household, for less cause than this. I opened the ground and swallowed them, he and his household, and Dathan and Abiram, and all their households. I made Miriam a leper white as snow for less insubordinate ways, and she was a prophetess of the Lord and a sister to Moses. I burnt to death the sons of Aaron, who were priests, enveloped them in flame for a mere breach of hieratic conduct. Then what shall I do with you, Gideon, who shout at the Lord? (*Gideon squatting down on his haunches, still sullen.*)

GIDEON. I did not mean to shout.

THE ANGEL. I will not make you king over these people, for they shall see a king and forget about the Lord. They shall bow down to the king, and they shall not bow down to me. They will seek blessings from this king who cannot bless and fear this king who cannot frighten. Therefore I am the king over Israel, and the people shall bow down to me and fear me and seek my blessings. Surely, this is clear to you.

GIDEON. (*Mutters, sulking.*) Yes, yes, yes.

THE ANGEL. Oh, Gideon, let us not quarrel, for I love you.

GIDEON. I am in this sullen temper. I cannot seem to master it.

THE ANGEL. (*Crossing to Gideon and squatting beside him.*) You are worn with battle and marching. Then rest and let me see your true and amiable self next time we meet.

GIDEON. Do not be kind to me, my Lord. I shall only cry.

THE ANGEL. I said I shall exalt you above your fellows, and I shall. I vowed seventy sons to you; well, then, know that both your wives at home are now with child. Indeed, from this moment, all women shall plead to be your wives. Now that should please you. (*Gideon works up a shallow smile.*) Come, give me your hand. If I have given you some hurt, then take my hand and show me it is over with. (*Gideon, keeping his eyes petulantly down, lets the Angel take his hand and clasp it.*) Now, eat and rest; then go and smite the elders of this city, as I have instructed you, preserve not one. (*Gideon nods bleakly.*)

GIDEON. I would be left to myself now, my Lord.

THE ANGEL. Of course. (*He stands.*) I shall wait for you beside your tent at Ophrah. Before I go, will you not say you love me?

GIDEON. (*Mutters.*) I love you, God.

THE ANGEL. (*Sighs.*) Peace be with you, Gideon.

GIDEON. Peace be with you, my Lord. (*The Angel turns and exits down the ladder. Gideon bows his head and murmurs.*) Hallowed, sanctified, glorious, magnified, holy is the Lord. The Lord is perfect, he shall reign for ever and ever. (*He looks up, notes the Angel is gone. He stands, regards the stage of bowed backs. He is still in a black temper.*) Rise up! Rise up! I asked for food. Bring me water to bathe my feet. (*He indicates the bodies of Zebah and Zalmunna.*) And get rid of that carrion there. (*The people rise quickly. Hand maidens scurry up from the pit, bringing steaming meat, bowls of fruit and skins of wine to where the*

53

various captains are gathered. Gideon crosses to them.) Here, give me that skin of wine before you've drunk it all.

SHILLEM. (*Giving a skin of wine to Gideon.*) I was telling these Ephraimites, O Gideon, how last night at Karkor four Midianites descended on me in a bunch . . . (*He sees Gideon is in no mood for campfire stories and breaks off. Orpah has made herself Gideon's handmaiden. As he stands, scowling and swilling the wine, she unwraps his girdle and unwinds his ankle-length outer garment.*)

GIDEON. (*Mutters.*) It is not easy to be loved by God, I tell you that.

SHILLEM. What did you say, my lord Gideon?

GIDEON. Perhaps, you chiefs and princes think it is a splendid state to be loved by God; well, it is not. Do this, do that, such-and-such, so-and-so, constant demands, and what does one get for a thank-you? Ah, well, let us not speak of it any more. It only puts me in a fury. (*Gideon wrenches a chunk of meat from the bowl beside him and champs angrily at it. His ugly mood has cast rather a pall over all the others onstage. During the above speech, the maiden Orpah is called to one side by her father, the Elder Ozni. By dumb show, they make clear a plot is hatching. She suddenly whirls away from her father, her eyes flashing. She gives her tambourine a good whack and stamps her foot. Then she turns her full voluptuous attention on Gideon who has looked briefly up at her. Orpah lifts her face high and chants out in the high-pitched manner of Oriental song.*)

ORPAH.

> Wherefore do they lament, the virgins of Succoth?
> Let them weep for their fathers tomorrow.
> Rejoice, ye maidens of Israel!
> Rejoice and dance at the gates!
> See the blood of Midian!
> See how it gels in the dust!
> Rejoice, ye virgins of Israel!
> It is not thy blood in the dust!
> Recall how they ripped thee, Virgins.
> They defiled thee on the highways.
> Then rejoice, O Virgin of Israel!
> Thy blood remains clean for thy marriage.
> On the night of thy wedding, O Virgin,

54

shall thy blood for the first time be seen.
Thy husband shall flourish thy nightdress
and shout: "See the stains of innocence!"
Sing praise, O maidens, to Gideon!
Let thy husbands cry out: "Amen!"
Hosanna!

(*She smashes her tabret and leaps into savage dance. The Soldiers and Captains, needless to say, find her dance diverting.*)

SHILLEM. The hot sun and the wine and the dancing rouse the blood, do they not?

SHETHULAH. Aye.

GIDEON. Aye. (*Gideon watches the voluptuous dance with evident interest. Suddenly, with a swoop, Orpah sinks to the ground at Gideon's feet and remains huddled, trembling, prostrate. The Elder, Ozni, cannily noting the appreciation Gideon entertains for his daughter, scrambles closer to Gideon, pulling along with him the other two Elders whose necks are joined to his by a rope.*)

OZNI. Oh, my lord Gideon, I see my maiden daughter Orpah here is pleasing in your eye. Could you think of her—well, in a manner of speaking—as a sacrifice of atonement that we wretched men of Succoth offer up to you? Take my daughter here as wife, great Gideon, and be merciful with us and spare our lives.

SECOND ELDER. Spare us, my lord. (*Gideon sullenly regards the piteous old faces staring at him, takes a good look at the girl again, considers the suggestion for a moment.*)

GIDEON. Well, it is an interesting idea. (*He throws Orpah aside.*) But it can't be done. It was the word of the Lord that you must die; I cannot gainsay God. (*He turns glowering to his Captains, fairly drunk now.*) I spoke to the Lord about this, you know. I said: "They are such piteous old wretches, and they are our own brothers. Must I kill them?" "Oh," spoke the Lord, "indeed you must!" And he told me some wild farrago of things concerning the temporal inadequacies of man, now, was and is and all manner of things like that. Oh, let me say again, it is not an easy thing to love God. One must transcend all the frailties of man. Do you not think I would like this juicy doxy here for a wife? But even that is denied me. (*He seizes another skin of wine, takes a long swallow, and squats down on his haunches, belligerently drunk.*) I would ask of you, have I done well by the Lord?

SHETHULAH. Indeed you have.

55

GIDEON. Is there anyone here—I protest, is there anyone here who has ever heard me reprehend the Lord in any way?

SHILLEM. You have praised his name with every breath.

GIDEON. Well, then, what comes of this? I spoke with the Lord, and said: "The people think of me as their king, and I think it sensible that I should be king over these people. All other peoples have kings. There are kings in Tyre, Byblos, Boetia, in every Phoenician city, and the Egyptians indeed have had a full pedigree of pharaohs. They are well into their twenty-third dynasty by now.

HEZEKIAH. Twentieth.

GIDEON. Twentieth? Well, twentieth then. It does not belittle the argument. The point is, great empires are in the making in Asshur and in Babylon. Shall we always be the subject people?

MALCHIEL. (*Showing interest for the first time.*) And let the people say:

THE CAPTAINS. Amen.

GIDEON. In these words did I speak to the Lord: "Shall we not be a mighty nation too? May I not sit upon a throne as well as Tiglath-Pileser? Let Syria raise bowls of silver tribute above their heads to me! We are the crossroads of Asia here! Let the caravans from Aram pay duty on Gideon's highways!"

MALCHIEL. And let the people say:

THE CAPTAINS. Amen!

GIDEON. I would make a good king, I think.

SHILLEM. Oh, and I might be your vizier.

GIDEON. Well, you shall have to do without your vizierate and I without my crown. For these ambitions are vanity and show a lack of faith in God. (*Crossing* D.) The Lord brushed the whole idea aside and terrified me with horrible deaths for just the mentioning of it. (*Malchiel drops suddenly to one knee before Gideon, his zealot's eyes glowing.*)

MALCHIEL. Be our king, Gideon, and rule over us. This is the moment now to take the crown. The victory over Midian does make the other kings of Canaan tremble at your name. You have but to show your might of twenty thousand men before the gates of Megiddo or of Dor, and the Girgashite kings will fall in the dust before you and pay you tribute.

SHETHULAH. The Jebusites rule Jerusalem and the Amorites Beth-Shean. But stretch forth your palm, and these kings will put their cities in it.

GIDEON. Nay, nay, my captains, do not press me.

MALCHIEL. Does not all Israel cry out for a king? We shall be as a nation among nations. What say you, captain of Ephraim?

SHETHULAH. Let him be our king and rule over us.

MALCHIEL. What say you, chief of Naphtali?

SHILLEM. Let him be our king.

MALCHIEL. (*Standing.*) And my brother here and I are Asher. Reuben and Gad sit twenty thousand strong at the foot of the hill. Will Judah say nay to his redeemer? Will not Benjamin cry out: "Amen." You will give the Sea back to Zebulun and return Dan's inheritance wrenched from him by the Philistines. There will be peace again in Israel, and travelers will not fear the highways. For you will be "the Good King Gideon," and the land shall prosper. And let the people say:

ALL. Amen! (*Gideon sits crosslegged on the skins, his head bowed, the cynosure of all eyes. He looks up, deeply moved.*)

GIDEON. (*Gently.*) Nay, I will not rule over you, and my son will not rule over you; the Lord will rule over you. (*He rises and regards the assembled host around and below him.*) You shall love the Lord your God with all your soul and with all your heart and with all your might, for he is in truth our king, and we need no other. (*To his Captains.*) I have been insolent and have made the Lord unattractive in your eyes with my grumbling. (*He turns back to all the people, raises his hands high.*) Come, let us give offering up to God. We have taken much spoil; this is the portion I ask for myself: give me all the golden rings Midian wore in his ears and all the golden crescents Midian hung about the necks of his camels. I shall melt these golden things and make a sacred golden garment as a gift to the Lord. I shall set it on a high place by my tent, and in the sun it shall be seen for many miles. All who see it shall think of the Lord and remember his great victory. And let the people say:

ALL. Amen!

GIDEON. Give me my spear! The spirit of the Lord is upon me, and I shall kill these elders! (*Malchiel puts Gideon's spear into his hand. Gideon turns sharply, face set, and strides to where Ozni and the two other prostrate Elders are still hunched over on their knees, backs bowed in abject fear. Gideon raises the spear above his head and cries out in a mighty voice.*) The Lord our God is a wrathful God! His name is the Great and the Mighty and the

57

Terrible God, the Devouring God! Let not his wrath be raised against you as with these taunting men! (*He stands a moment, spear upraised and then a look of horror crosses his face. Slowly he brings the spear down and lets it dangle from his hand. He stands a moment, trembling with a kind of dread.*) I cannot do it. Let them live, Shillem, scourge them if you will with whips, with briars of the wilderness and thorns. For surely man must have more meaning than this. (*He shuffles disconsolately, even guiltily, a few steps away, casting a nervous look up to heaven and throwing spear off R.*)

SHILLEM. Well then, soldiers, go gather me briars from the wilderness and thorns and make a scourge for me. (*He nudges Ozni gently.*) Well, it is better than being killed, isn't it?

OZNI. (*Delight slowly spreading across his face.*) Yes. I suppose it is.

SHILLEM. (*To Gideon.*) The girl, Gideon, is yours, you know. (*Gideon, who had quite forgotten about Orpah, is delighted at being reminded. He sweeps her over his shoulder and carries her off. The people of Succoth, needless to say, spring up into great rejoicing. The Maidens smash tambourines and cymbals and dance enthusiastically. The Elders gaily sing out.*)

ELDERS.

> Hosanna! Hosanna!
> Sing glory to Gideon!
> His name is Merciful.
> He has redeemed us from Midian!
> The land is free, O Israel!
> Thy sons stand up, O Israel!
> Thy daughters dance, O Israel!
> Hosanna! Hosanna!

(*The Elders, escorted by Soldiers, start off L.; the Maidens dance, the stage is a scene of tumultuous revelry as the curtain comes quickly down.*)

END OF SCENE ONE

"And Gideon made an ephod of it and put it in his city, in
Ophrah; and all Israel played the harlot after it there, and
it became a snare to Gideon and to his family."

ACT II

SCENE 2

*The same as Act I, Scene 1, by the tents of Joash. It is
two days later.*

AT RISE: *The Angel is striding about the stage, glowering
and furious. He looks down the road to Schechem.*

THE ANGEL. (*At the terebinth tree.*) Ah, here he comes, hugging
to his chest the sacred golden garment he has made for me. Oh, he
shall know my wrath, indeed he shall. (*Enter Gideon, huffing and
puffing, holding the golden ephod to his chest with both hands. It is
crudely made but recognizable as a simple waist-length garment
with shoulder-straps, and it glitters and glistens handsomely. Orpah
follows a few wifely paces behind, robed and veiled, and carrying
a large bundle of her belongings on her head. The Angel regards
Gideon's entrance with a cold eye and says in an icy tone.*) The
Lord is with you, O mighty man of valor.
GIDEON. (*Startled.*) Oh! Peace be with you, my Lord. (*He sets
the golden ephod down atop the altar* u.) This is for you, my
Lord. I fashioned it myself. My Lord, I must have some few words
with you, but first let me make my presence known to my father
and my wives. Oh, here stands my new wife Orpah the daughter
of Ozni. Uncover your face, my wife, so that the Lord may look
upon you. Here, here, he stands by the tree here. (*Orpah lowers
her veil and turns blankly to the tree.*)
THE ANGEL. (*Coldly.*) Very handsome.
GIDEON. Yes. Well, let me go embrace my father and make my
presence known. I hope my gift finds favor in your eye.
THE ANGEL. Go and seek your father.
GIDEON. Yes, well, in a moment then. (*He takes Orpah's arm*

59

and starts for the tent.) He is invisible to you then, too. (*Orpah nods, looks nervously back to the terebinth tree.*) He is in a black temper. (*Joash comes bursting out of the tent.*)

JOASH. He is here! He is here among us! Come forth to greet him! O, my son, come let me embrace you. (*From out of the tent now pour Tirzah, Mahlah, Hoglah, Milcah, Abinoab and Jether, Gideon's son. They all stand at the tent flap staring in mute adoration at the returning hero. Joash embraces Gideon.*) Oh, my son, what honor you have brought to this house! The people of Abiezer are waiting for us now up on the threshing hill. Now, that you have come, we shall start the festival of Summer Fruits. Oh, Gideon, I am most blessed of fathers. Let water be brought that he may bathe his feet.

GIDEON. My father, this is a Gadite woman who is my wife. Her name is Orpah daughter of Ozni of the house of Eliasaph, a princely house. Give her your blessing and make her welcome in your tent.

JOASH. (*To Orpah, bowing low at his feet.*) Rise up, my daughter, take off your veil. You are in your own home.

GIDEON. (*Embracing Hoglah.*) My mother, let me embrace you. (*To Tirzah and Mahlah.*) My wives, this is the Gadite Orpah. Bring water that she may bathe her feet and drink. She is dear to me; honor her.

JOASH. Sit, my son, and let us attend you. (*Skins have been spread on the ground, R. C. Gideon and Orpah sit on them and have their feet bathed and are served cakes and water. Gideon looks anxiously back to the Angel; then tries to give his attention to his family.*)

GIDEON. These other ladies here are the widows of my brothers. This is my son, Jether, a pensive boy. His uncles call him donkey as they once called me. Well, you shall have sweeter names now. You are the only son of Gideon.

MAHLAH. Nay, nay, my lord. Oh, let my lord be told.

JOASH. Your wife Mahlah is with child again.

TIRZAH. And I do think the same, my lord. I too have passed my time.

GIDEON. (*Scowls, darts a nervous look at the Angel who snaps his fingers twice.*) Yea, God did promise me seventy sons. (*Turns back to Jether with a gentle smile and takes the boy's hand.*) But this is Jether, my first-born, who shall be a prince in Manasseh after me and whose opinion I hold dear. (*The boy stares at him in open-mouthed adulation.*)

JOASH. Oh, my son, we have heard such stories of your gallantry in war. Every passing soldier adds fifty to the host of Midianites you have slain.

GIDEON. Oh, I slew a few perhaps. (*The Angel snorts and throws up his hands.*)

THE ANGEL. Oh! (*Gideon turns to the Angel, his face appealing for indulgence, but he receives only a baleful glare.*)

GIDEON. (*Turning sadly back to his son.*) In truth, I killed no Midianites at all. These stories you have heard are but the usual legends of the battlefield.

JOASH. Your father was the general, boy. He stands behind and regards the course of things so that he may direct the overall tactic and maneuver.

GIDEON. Yes, yes, that is true, of course.

JOASH. It was your father who conceived the plan to stampede the Midianite cattle with lamps and trumpets.

GIDEON. Ah, there, of course, I must take the credit, and— (*He looks back to the Angel, who glowers at him again and gives vocal reaction.*) Well, even this was not my doing. The Lord our God instructed me what to do; I merely did it. (*The boy, Jether, is obviously disappointed by this, and Gideon pained by his disappointment.*)

JOASH. But there passed through here just yesterday a prince of Asher whose name was Hezekiah the son of Immah who expounded to us for many hours on the war and said that Gideon was among the great generals.

GIDEON. Did he say that indeed?

JOASH. Aye, and this Hezekiah is well-known as a scholar and knows many things.

GIDEON. Oh, indeed, he predicts the eclipses of the moon and has measured the ecliptic of the sun as it revolves around the earth.

JOASH. And this Hezekiah described the history of the war, and indeed God did not enter into it at all. "We are all men of reason here," he said, "and need not explain all things in supernatural ways. The savage will say God gave us into the hand of the Midianites," said Hezekiah, "but was it not in fact the economic conditions of drought in the desert that drove the Midianites upon us." And then he said: "Was it the spirit of God that aroused the tribes

61

of Israel to rebel, or was it not rather the need to protect our growing cities, our increase in caravan trade, and the beginnings of our mercantile interests? Is the panic of the one hundred and twenty thousand Midianites so hard to understand when one realizes the superstitious spirit of the men of Midian? For these were a primitive people with a crumbling social fabric. All that was needed was a bold and ingenious general who could exploit these weaknesses of Midian." And, indeed, Gideon, that was you. (*Gideon considers this explanation a moment.*)

GIDEON. (*Standing, crossing* D. C.) Well, it is not altogether illogical, is it?

JOASH. "Indeed," said this Hezekiah, "who is this Yahweh of Gideon's? Has anyone seen him or heard his words? Only Gideon." It was Hezekiah's contention, Gideon, that Yahweh was a masterful fiction you created to inspirit the troops.

GIDEON. (*Eagerly, crossing to Joash.*) Now, how did his reasoning go again? It was the economic conditions prevailing in the desert of Havilah that . . .

THE ANGEL. (*Roaring.*) Gideon! Will you countenance this pomander of utter nonsense? (*The eager smile disappears from Gideon's face, and he sighs unhappily.*)

GIDEON. Ah. (*He regards his son anxiously.*) It is none of it true, my son. It was the Lord our God who gave us into the hand of Midian, for we had bowed down to false gods, and it was the Lord our God who redeemed us by the strength of his hand alone. Yea, though none of you may see nor hear him, he is here among us now, and I see and hear him. There is no honor due me at all, but that I am the device of God. (*Jether, embarrassed by his father's humility, lowers his eyes and shuffles away* u. *Gideon watches him go anxiously.*)

JOASH. (*Now suddenly terrified.*) He is here among us, did you say, the Lord our God?

GIDEON. (*Watching his son.*) Aye. (*Joash immediately prostrates himself to the ground as do all the others onstage, excepting Jether—who has suddenly noticed the glistening ephod on the altar* u.—*and Gideon who is watching him. The boy approaches the ephod to examine it.*)

THE ANGEL. Do not let him touch it, Gideon. It is a thing of God, and he will die. (*The boy reaches out to touch the ephod.*)

GIDEON. (*Crying out.*) Do not touch it! It is holy! You will die!

62

JOASH. My son, you have carried it in your hands for twenty miles.

GIDEON. I have given it to God, and it is holy now. Not you nor I nor the Levite priests of God may touch it, for it is a holy thing.

JOASH. (*Looking up terrified from his prostrate position.*) Behold the sacred golden garment Gideon has made for God!

GIDEON. (*Stands and faces the Angel.*) There is no putting it off, my Lord, but I must have a word with you.

THE ANGEL. And I with you, Gideon.

GIDEON. (*To his father.*) My father, go and make ready for the festival on the hill. Let my new wife be taken to my tent. Leave me here alone. I must speak with the Lord. (*The others rise quickly and exit off into the tent. For a moment, the stage is silent, Gideon D. in frowning concentration and the Angel U. waiting in cold anger. Then Gideon turns to the Angel.*) My Lord, we have always spoken plainly with each other.

THE ANGEL. I am not pleased with this golden ephod you have made. (*Crosses D. L. C.*) It is a pagan thought to think your God wears golden undercoats.

GIDEON. I fashioned it for love of you, my Lord.

THE ANGEL. (*Crosses behind Gideon.*) Indeed, you did not, but as a wily gift to turn aside my wrath. You betrayed me at Succoth, Gideon. I charged you to slay the elders, and you did not. Shall you say who shall die and who shall live? I am the Lord. I kill, and I make alive. Shall you gainsay me? Have you seen the end of time? Do you know the beginning and what came before that? Do you know whence you rose? Do you know where you go? Are you God now that you give life where I have taken it away?

GIDEON. I pitied the old men, my Lord.

THE ANGEL. And I watched you sit there now, greedily believing all of Hezekiah's chimera and claptrap about the socio-economic conditions in the desert of Havilah—you, who have seen the Lord face-to-face and beheld his wonders.

GIDEON. Well, Hezekiah is well-spoken of as a scholar. He knows all about the ecliptic of the sun as it revolves around the earth.

THE ANGEL. (*Crosses U.*) The sun does not revolve around the earth, you imbecile; the earth revolves about the sun.

63

GIDEON. Oh, that is patent nonsense, my Lord. The sun obviously revolves around the earth.

THE ANGEL. (*Crosses* L.) Oh! I do not know how I bear with you!

GIDEON. (*Crying out.*) Oh, my Lord, let me go!

THE ANGEL. Let you go?

GIDEON. We have made a covenant of love between us, you and I. Release me from that covenant.

THE ANGEL. (*Crosses* D. L.) Are you suggesting some sort of divorce between your God and you?

GIDEON. We make an ill-matched pair, my Lord. You surely see we never meet but tempers rise between us. It is too much for me, this loving God. I cannot manage it. I am a plain man and subject to imperfect feelings. I shall betray you many times, and you shall rise in wrath against me and shall punish me with mighty penalties, and I cannot continue in this way, my Lord. Oh, let me say it plainly. I do not love you, Lord, and it is unreasonable to persist with each other when there is no love.

THE ANGEL. (*Startled.*) You do not love me?

GIDEON. (*Crosses to the Angel, kneels.*) I tried to love you, but it is too much for me. You are too vast a concept for me. To love you, God, one must be a god himself. I did not kill the elders of Succoth, and I shall tell you why. I raised my spear above their heads, but in that moment I felt a shaft of terror that chills me even now. It was as if the nakedness of all things was exposed to me, and I saw myself and all men for what we truly are, suspensions of matter, flailing about for footholds in the void, all the while slipping back screaming into endless suffocations. That is the truth of things, I know, but I cannot call it truth. It is too hideous, an intolerable state of affairs. I cannot love you, God, for it makes me a meaningless thing.

THE ANGEL. (*Thoroughly exasperated, crosses* R.) Oh!

GIDEON. (*Rises, crosses* D. C.) My Lord, it is elemental in me to aspire to be greater than myself. This is your own doing, for you gave me passion that I might raise myself to you. You have uncovered your nakedness before me. How shall I think myself an aimless brute now?

THE ANGEL. (*Crosses to Gideon.*) I meant you to love me, but you are merely curious. You have no feeling for me then at all?

64

GIDEON. I fear you, God. I am in mortal dread of you. Perhaps, that is the only love a man can give his god.

THE ANGEL. (*Deeply hurt, sits bundle* L.) What shall we do then, Gideon?

GIDEON. Let me go, God.

THE ANGEL. Let you go—whatever does that mean? Gideon, there is no divorce from God. (*Rises.*) I am truth and exist. You cannot deny that I am. I stand palpably here before you, as real as rock, a very actual thing with whom you have commerced face-to-face.

GIDEON. Aye, my Lord. I see you and hear you. So I beg of you, my Lord—go from my sight. Make not your presence known to me again that I might say: "God is a dream, a name, a thought, but not a real thing."

THE ANGEL. But I am a real thing.

GIDEON. I would pretend that you were not. (*The Angel is a little startled at this.*)

THE ANGEL. Let me review this. You would pretend God is not although you know that he is, so that you might be a significant creature which you know you are not. Oh! This is beyond even God's understanding! (*Crosses* C.) And you do not love me! I found you a mournful farmer, and I have loved you and raised you up and uncovered your soul and gave you many satisfactions. And now you turn on me like a disgruntled husband and would send me packing back to my father's tent. This was not the case when you needed me, was it? O! What protestations of ardor you made then! And I was susceptible enough to think the man did love me. I have been too kind with you, indeed I have! If fear is all the love you have for me, then you shall fear me, Gideon. You betrayed me at Succoth. You have given the life of men greater value than the word of God. Behold then, Gideon! Know that there is a God, and that his will is all there is. As I blessed you for your love, so shall I punish you for your infidelity. You did not slay the seven and seventy elders of Succoth. Then, the seventy sons I promised you shall die in their stead.

GIDEON. (*Sinks to the ground, stricken.*) Oh!

THE ANGEL. They shall die in bitterness by each other's hands. As you contend with me, so shall they contend between themselves.

GIDEON. Oh, God, this is most cruel!

THE ANGEL. It seems just weight to me. Behold then, Gideon.

65

I give life and I take it away. I bless, and I punish. I am pleased, and I rise in wrath. This is the law of the universe; there is no other. (*Crosses up to perch.*)

GIDEON. (*Shriveled now into a terrified ball on the ground.*) Oh, my Lord, I cannot continue in this way! (*Gideon, frozen in terror, huddles hunched against further lashes of punishment. After a moment, he looks slowly up, his face drawn into an expression of intense anguish. His eye is caught by the appearance of Jether, who has shuffled out of the tent and would come to his father but sees that the latter is on his knees in profound prayer.*) Spare me at least my one only son, my Lord. I have never known his love. His mother taught him her contempt, but now, I think, he might love me, and I would like that, God. (*Joash, Orpah and the other women now come out of the tent, stop at the sight of Gideon, on his knees in prayer, and stand silently and a little frightened.*) Behold mine own small world of people there. Could I not pretend there is some reason for their being here? Pretend, my Lord, no more than that. Let me have at least some bogus value.

THE ANGEL. (*Gently.*) I am truth, Gideon. I cannot vary. (*Gideon bows his head, utterly crushed. Then he slowly looks up again, but apparently does not see the Angel immediately.*)

GIDEON. My Lord?

THE ANGEL. Yes? (*Gideon looks around the stage.*)

GIDEON. God?

THE ANGEL. I am by the wine-press now.

GIDEON. God?

THE ANGEL. Here, Gideon, by the press.

GIDEON. Are you still here?

THE ANGEL. Here, over here.

GIDEON. (*Standing.*) Ah, yes, you do seem blurred. (*Crosses to the Angel.*) My Lord, I asked you one small thing, that I might delude myself with some spurious grandeur.

THE ANGEL. And I answered: "No, it will not do." You want the universe to please your eye, Gideon, and not mine. You would be God yourself. (*Gideon crosses D.*) Hear me well, O Hebrew. I am a jealous God and brook no other gods, not even you. Why have I come here at all but to put an end to false idols? You have done well in pulling down the effigies of Ba-al, but do not think to set yourself up on their empty altars. Do not make a cult of man, not even in fancy.

66

GIDEON. (*Looking around.*) My Lord? My Lord?

THE ANGEL. Attend me, Gideon, and mark my words.

GIDEON. (*Crosses* U.) My Lord?

THE ANGEL. Where are you looking, Gideon? I am here.

GIDEON. My Lord, where are you gone?

THE ANGEL. Here! I stand here! By the wine-press here! I have not moved!

GIDEON. (*Crosses* D. C.) My Lord, please speak to me. We are not finished.

THE ANGEL. What is this game?

GIDEON. My Lord!

THE ANGEL. I stand right here!

GIDEON. Where are you, Lord? The matter is not finished!

THE ANGEL. (*Crying out.*) O Gideon, do not forsake me!

GIDEON. God! Where are you, God? I cannot see you, God! You have not answered what I asked you! (*At this point, Abimelech and Helek come hurrying in from* U. L. *behind the tent.*)

ABIMELECH. Ah! There he is! They said they saw him on the road!

HELEK. Oh, Gideon, how good to have you back. (*Joash peremptorily admonishes the new arrivals to silence. Indeed, Gideon's scene with the Angel has been watched with mingled dread and confusion by his family. Now, Gideon stands* C., *as if transfixed, staring up to the heavens. The Angel, who had turned exasperatedly away at the interruption, now moves intently to Gideon, as angry as only a scorned god can be.*)

THE ANGEL. Gideon, I pray you, do not scorn me! I will not be so cast off out of hand. You leave this house, return not to it ever. For I have had my fill of your betrayals, your sordid harlotries with other gods. And now there are new strumpets on the highway. Well, go then to those painted dialectics and libertine philosophies and logics that wait along the road for gulls like you, and, for a shekel, shrilly promise you the secret sensuality of time and space. You will be ravished, fleeced, and soon abandoned in some red-threaded hovel of despair. Then do not hope that God awaits at home when with ragged beard the penitent returns. Turn not your face from me! Beware my wrath! There is no divorce from God! Hear that! God gives no divorce, but just his curse! (*Gideon, to all effects and purposes, has not heard a word.*)

GIDEON. I do not see you, God, nor hear you now. What was

67

between us now is done. And let the people say: "Amen." (*A long silence fills the stage. After a moment, Joash calls tentatively to his son.*)

JOASH. My son, the house of Abiezer waits to honor you on the threshing hill. (*By the wine-press, the Angel looks sadly at his hands.*)

THE ANGEL. Gideon, I am the Lord your God who brought you out of the land of Egypt. I broke the bars of your yoke and made you stand erect. Will you spurn my statutes? Will you break my covenant?

GIDEON. (*His eyes closed against the Angel's words.*) I must aspire, God.

THE ANGEL. (*Thundering.*) Then I shall do this to you and to all of Israel! I will make your heavens like iron and your earth like brass! I will scatter you among the nations! (*With great effort, Gideon forces his attention back to the others onstage.*)

GIDEON. (*To his family.*) Well, come, then, let us go to the festival.

THE ANGEL. I will unsheath the sword after you! Your land shall be a desolation, and your cities shall be a waste!

GIDEON. (*Forcing his attention on the ephod.*) I shall put on this golden garment and wear it to the festival. (*Gideon, with set jaw, starts u. to the ephod. The Angel raises his arm in lordly threat.*)

THE ANGEL. (*Thundering.*) Gideon! Do not touch it! This thing is mine!

GIDEON. (*Whirls and cries out.*) O God! I cannot believe in you! If you love me, let me believe at least in mine own self! If you love me, God! (*The Angel stares at Gideon with a face strained by deep emotion. Then his upraised arm falls to his side.*)

THE ANGEL. I love you, Gideon! (*Gideon promptly turns and takes hold of the ephod.*)

GIDEON. Father, help me to put it on. (*With the apprehensive help of Joash and of his son, Jether, Gideon contrives to get the weighty ephod over his head and down onto his body.*) What a heavy thing it is. (*The Angel, still deeply moved, looks up, smiles.*)

THE ANGEL. Oh, indeed it is.

ABIMELECH. (*Staring in awe at the gold-clad Gideon.*) We all wait to hear you tell the miracle of God's victory over Midian. (*Gideon turns slowly to the Elders.*)

GIDEON. A miracle? Why do you call it that? (*Wrapping his*

arms around his uncles, he leads the small procession of his family off R.) Nay, my uncles, the war with Midian was not mysterious, but only the inevitable outgrowth of historico-economic, socio-psychological and cultural forces prevailing in these regions. (*They al exeunt off* R. *to attend the festival of summer fruits on the hill. The Angel has watched them go with amusement. Now, he cannot resist bursting into laughter.*)

THE ANGEL. Oh, it is amusing. (*He moves* D. *and regards the audience, quite cheerful now. Behind him, the stage is now empty. After a moment, he recites:*)

> God no more believes it odd
> that man cannot believe in God.
> Man believes the best he can,
> which means, it seems, belief in man.
> Then let him don my gold ephod
> and let him be a proper god.
> Well, let him try it anyway.
> With this conceit, we end the play.

(*The Angel bows. The lights black out.*)

THE END

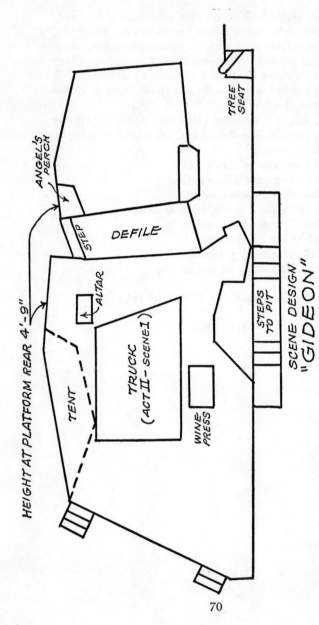

HEIGHT AT PLATFORM REAR 4'-9"

ANGEL'S PERCH

STEP

DEFILE

ALTAR

TENT

TRUCK (ACT II – SCENE I)

WINE PRESS

STEPS TO PIT

TREE SEAT

SCENE DESIGN "GIDEON"

NOTE: This ground plan is for the New York production of GIDEON, and although most elements called for in the script are shown in this ground plan, the positioning may vary from the script description. The entire stage left hill area was built as a seesaw so that in Act I, Scenes 2 and 3 the ridge (or high part of the hill) was down stage, while for the other scenes it was upstage. For Act II, Scene 1, a truck (as shown) was used in place of the threshing floor. The construction of the stage right platform (hill) enabled the truck to roll into position and off again. No terebinth tree was used.

PROPERTY LIST

Bundles of wheat (3)
Stick to beat out wheat
Cover for beating out wheat
Burlap sling for wheat
Sacrifice (kid) off R.
Spears (5)
Tamborines (5)
Foot bowl and cloth
Silver boat horn
Several shields
War bow
Wine jugs (3)
Wine bottles (3)
Wine sacks (2)
Several bundles of assorted sizes and shapes
Several baskets
Small wooden bowls for drinking (5)
Baking tray with cakes
Steer horn
Cloth and cover for slain Midian kings
Grapes in bowl
Whip
Finger cymbals (4)
Heads in bag (2)
Broken altar
Shield, snake and water bottle on bundle
Large fruit tray
Loose fruit
Tent
Altar
Wine press
Ephod
Knife in scabbard (Joash)
Small branch (I-2)
Torches (flambeaux) (3)
Leather water skin
Bowls of meat
Animal skins
Scimitar, in scabbard

GENERAL LIGHTING

Act I

Scene 1

The lighting in this scene gives the impression of bright sunlight, heat, and dryness. THE ANGEL on his perch up left center and on top of the left hill is lit in bright white light, and white light is also used for GIDEON'S prophecy speeches at the end of the scene. Playing areas used by THE ANGEL and GIDEON are generally more brightly lit than the remainder of the stage. Most colors used on both the stages and the cyclorama are ambers and white.

Scene 2

General lighting in this scene is much the same as the first scene with perhaps higher readings for the first part of the scene. As GIDEON alternates scenes between THE ANGEL and the CAPTAINS, these areas are raised and lowered in lighting levels. After the final departure of the Captains the stage begins to grow darker to represent evening and blue light is used. Special moon light is used on the KINGS OF MIDIAN and white light is used on THE ANGEL and GIDEON for the end of the scene. When THE ANGEL eclipses the moon the stage is made dark except for the lights on GIDEON and himself.

Scene 3

At the beginning of the scene the stage is darkly lit to represent night. Special areas are used for the opening scene between THE ANGEL and GIDEON and for the "love scene." At the end of this scene the stage becomes slowly brighter to represent dawn and the morning heat. The remainder of the scene is brightly lit in amber and white light.

Act II

Scene 1

Scene opens with much deep amber light on cyclorama and set, with down left area and pit step area more brightly lit. As GIDEON approaches platform (threshing floor) this area is brought into play and the level is raised and lowered as he leaves platform to talk with THE ANGEL and returns again. The platform area and area in front of platform are brightly lit during Orpah's dance and scene after dance. Again the general mood is of heat and dryness.

Scene 2

Lighting here is much the same as Scene 1, with special white light for THE ANGEL'S perch and amber light for the ephod. Area lighting is used during scenes between THE ANGEL and GIDEON, and as GIDEON begins to have difficulty in seeing THE ANGEL the stage gradually grows darker, until it is only dimly lit at GIDEON'S exit except for specials on THE ANGEL. Brighter stage left area lighting is used for THE ANGEL'S final speech.

COSTUME PLOT—NEW YORK PRODUCTION

ANGEL:
2 pairs of black tights
Black jersey under robe
Wig
Beard
Shoes

Scenes 1 thru 4:
Black and grey striped robe

Scene 5:
Black silk robe with large hood

GIDEON:
Athletic supporter
Loin cloth

Scene 1:
1 knee length belted tunic
Wig
Beard
Barefoot

Scene 2:
Skirt
Curaiss—removed during scene
Baldric
Sandals
Poniard
Leather vest—put on after the curaiss is removed

Scene 3:
Same, with the addition of:
  Vest
  Belt with scimitar

Scene 4:
Same as Scene 3

Scene 5:
Same as Scene 4

Golden Ephod (carried on stage and put on, on stage)

SHILLEM:

Scenes 2, 3 and 4 (no change)
Leather corset
Skirt
Costume dressing
Boots
Wig
Beard
War bow
Quiver
2 athletic supporters
1 loin cloth

MALCHIEL:

Scenes 2, 3 and 4 (no change)
Leather corset
Fur skirt
Wig
Beard
Sandals
Helmet
2 athletic supporters
Loin cloth
Spear
Scimitar

HEZEKIAH:

Scenes 2, 3 and 4 (no change)
Leather corset
Skirt
Wig
Beard
Boots
2 athletic supporters

74

1 loin cloth
Shield
Sling and stone pouch

JAHLEEL:

Scene 2:

Leather tunic
Skirt
Helmet
Sandals
Wig
Beard
2 athletic supporters
1 loin cloth
Broad sword and belt

OZNI:

Scene 4:
Robe
Prayer shawl
Sandals

JOASH:

Scenes 1 and 5:
Robe
Under robe
Sacrificial robe
Prayer shawl
Wig
Wig
Beard
Sandals

ABIMELECH:

Scenes 1 and 5:
Robe
Under robe
Shawl
Wig
Beard
Sandals

HELEK:

Scenes 1 and 5:
Robe
Under robe
Shawl
Hump
Wig
Beard
Sandal
Walking stick

SUCCOTH ELDERS II and III:
(Abimelech and Helek doubling)

Scene 4:
Robe over original under robe
Prayer shawl
Original sandals

ELDER III:
Change of beard
Rope for tying elders together

JETHER:

Scenes 1 and 5 (no change)
Leather shift
Wig
Sandals

SHETHULAH:

Scenes 3 and 4 (no change)
Robe
Leather corset
Skirt
Helmet
Sandals
Wig
Beard
2 athlethic supporters
Loin cloth
Whip

PURAH:

Scenes 2, 3 and 4 (no change)
Skirt

Sandals
Wig
Beard
2 athletic supporters
1 loin cloth
Large mattock

ZEBA:

Scene 2:
Robe
Under robe
Turban
Sandals
Wig
Beard
Jewelry

Scene 4:
Torn robe
Torn turban
Barefoot
Eye patch
Wig and beard

ZALMUNA:

Scene 2:
Robe
Turban
Sandals
Wig
Beard
Jewelry

Scene 4:
Torn robe
Torn turban
Barefoot
Wig and beard

SOLDIERS: I, II, III, IV
      (Zeba doubling)

Scenes 2, 3 and 4:
Leather corset
Skirt

Helmet
Sandals
Wig
Beard
1 loin cloth
2 athletic supporters

CAPTURED SOLDIERS:

Scene 3:
Bloody tunic
Barefoot
Gag in mouth
Same wig and beard as original
   costume

SLAVE DRIVER:

Scene 3:
Leather straps over black loin
   cloth

ORPHAH:

Scene 4:
Collar
Skirt
Veil
Sandals
Wig
Jewelry

Scene 5:
Robe
Shawl
Sandals
Wig

WOMEN OF MANASSEH:

Scenes 1 and 5:
Robe
Under robe
Shawl
Sandals
Wig

WOMEN OF SUCCOTH:
     (except Orpah u. s.)

76

Scene 4:

Under robe from Scene 1 and 5
Robe
Wig
Sandals from Scene 1 and 5

ÓRPAH U. S.:

Collar
Skirt
Veil
Wig
Sandals

New  PLAYS

New PLAYS

THE CREATION OF THE WORLD AND OTHER BUSINESS

THE LAST OF MRS. LINCOLN

STATUS QUO VADIS

DON JUAN

MYSTERY PLAY

DUCKS AND LOVERS

CONTINENTAL DIVIDE

THE DEATH AND LIFE OF SNEAKY FiTCH

WHISKEY

LET ME HEAR YOU WHISPER & THE LADIES SHOULD BE IN BED

THE OWL KILLER

THE REMARKABLE SUSAN

DRAMATISTS PLAY SERVICE, INC.

440 PARK AVENUE SOUTH   NEW YORK, N.Y. 10016